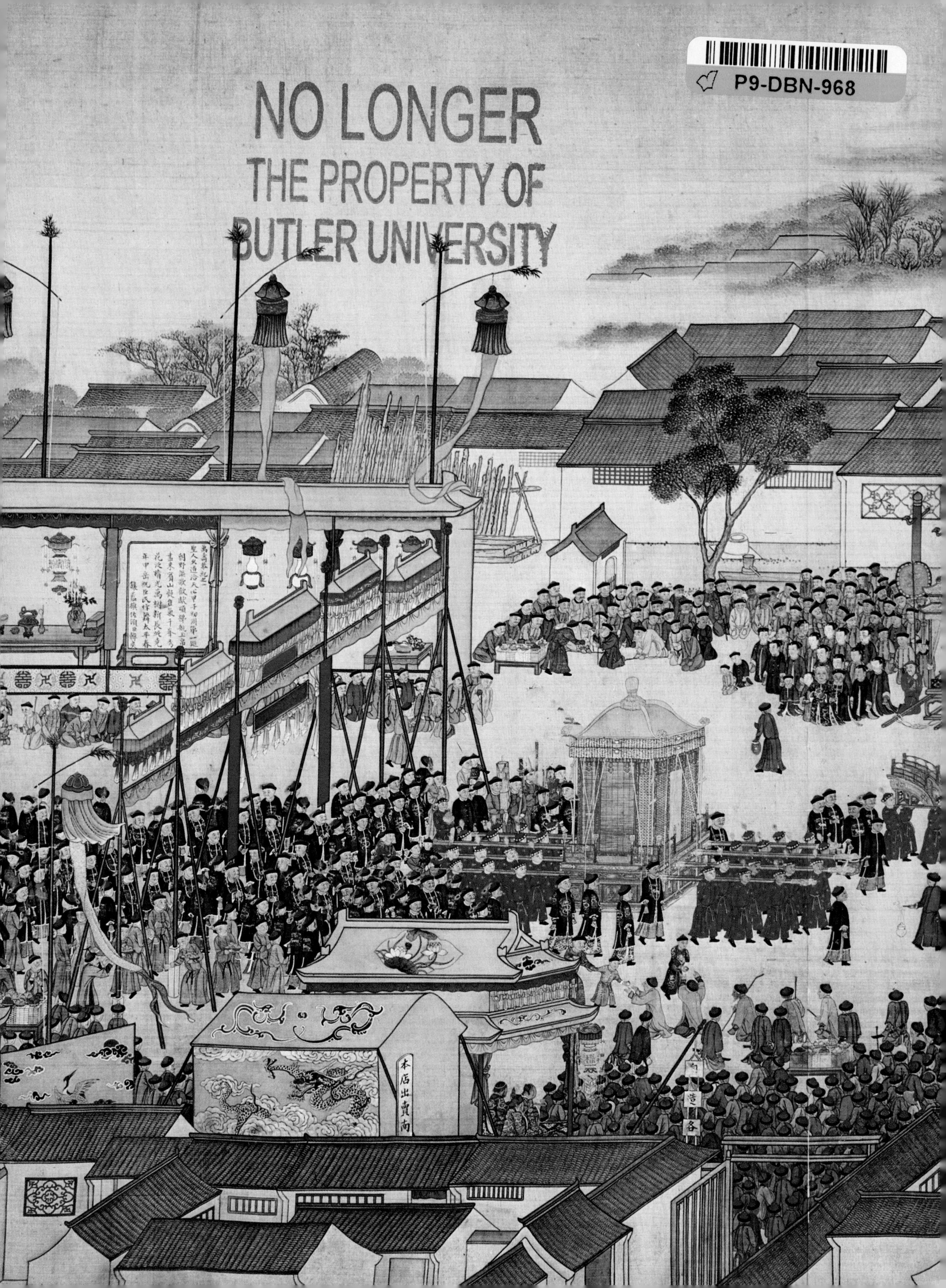

WONDERS OF MAN

THE FORBIDDEN CITY

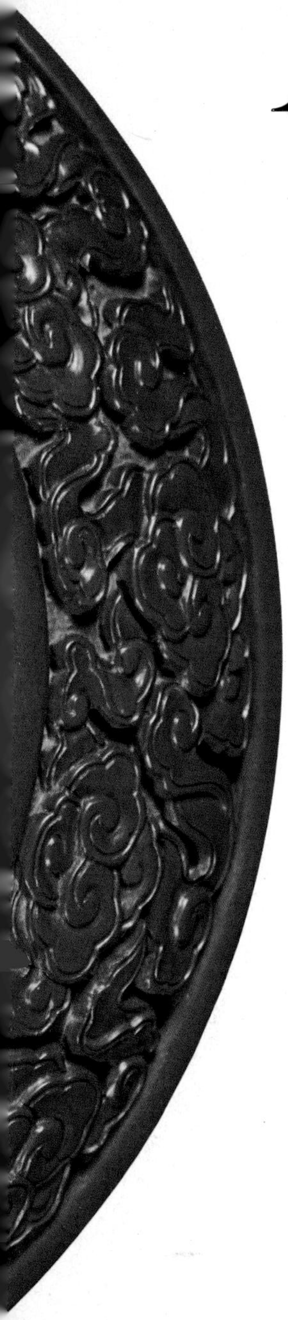

by Roderick MacFarquhar
and the Editors
of the Newsweek Book Division

NEWSWEEK, New York

NEWSWEEK BOOK DIVISION

JOSEPH L. GARDNER   *Editor*

Janet Czarnetzki   *Art Director*

Edwin D. Bayrd, Jr.   *Associate Editor*
Laurie P. Phillips   *Picture Editor*
Eva Galan   *Assistant Editor*
Kathleen Berger   *Copy Editor*
Susan Storer   *Picture Researcher*
Russell Ash   *European Correspondent*

ALAIN GARFIN   *Publisher*

WONDERS OF MAN

MILTON GENDEL   *Consulting Editor*

Mary Ann Joulwan   *Designer, The Forbidden City*

Endpapers:
*Borne on a curtained palanquin, the
Ch'ing dynasty emperor K'ang-hsi
enters Peking with his retinue.*

Title Page:
*Feet splayed and torso contorted, a
five-clawed imperial dragon writhes
atop a lacquered Ming dynasty box.*

Opposite:
*Buddhist emblems decorate the shaft
of this turquoise-and-gold scepter,
which once belonged to the
renowned eighteenth-century
emperor Ch'ien Lung.*

9th Printing 1981

ISBN: Clothbound Edition 0–88225–022–1
ISBN: Deluxe Edition 0–88225–023–X
Library of Congress Catalog Card No. 70–178708

Contents

Introduction

Throughout recorded history the peoples of China have systematically and emphatically turned their backs on the north — largely with good reason. Malign forces were said to reside in the north, and barbarian tribesmen were known to lurk there, rallying their forces for periodic attacks upon the peaceful, pastoral communities of the south. To shield themselves from the evil spirits that dwelt in the north, the Chinese oriented their homes and even their cities to the south; to ward off the marauding nomads of the steppe they erected the Great Wall along China's northwest frontier.

Ironically enough, the nomads who succeeded in breaching the wall frequently established vigorous, effective, and enduring administrations in the south. For these conqueror-dynasts the sere and barren North China plain was an ideal site for an imperial city, for it lay midway between the barbarians' grassy homeland and the fertile farmlands of the Yangtze valley. In all other respects, however, Peking was an illogical location for a national capital, and the perpetual problems of provisioning the inland city were to topple more than one regime. Despite these drawbacks, Peking was to emerge in the early fifteenth century as the cultural and administrative nexus of the entire realm. At the same time the capital's inner sanctum, the Forbidden City, was to evolve into a labyrinthine complex of airy audience halls, intimate private pavilions, secluded gardens, and sprawling courtyards — each distinctive, and all distinctly Chinese in both conception and detailing, as the view at left indicates.

In time the cloistered corridors of the Forbidden City were to become a virtual prison, one in which China's last emperors were sequestered. Isolated and insular, these hapless rulers clung so doggedly to outmoded traditions that they doomed the monarchy and brought their country to the brink of revolution in 1911. The ultimate, cataclysmic result of their folly — the protracted and bitter civil war between the followers of Chiang Kai-shek and those of Mao Tse-tung that culminated in a Communist victory in 1949 — was to reshape the entire society of China and throw wide the doors of the once-sacrosanct Forbidden City.

THE EDITORS

THE FORBIDDEN CITY
IN HISTORY

I

A Kingdom Lost for Love

Years later, when the rebellion had been suppressed and the T'ang dynasty had been restored to some of its former glory, the love of Yang Kuei-fei and the emperor Hsuan Tsung was celebrated as one of the greatest romances of all time. For Yang Kuei-fei, a famous T'ang poet wrote, the emperor neglected the three thousand lovely women who graced his court: "If she but turned her head and smiled, then were cast a hundred spells, and the powder and paint of the Six Palaces faded into nothing." The contemporaries of Yang Kuei-fei, "Precious Consort" Yang, also paid tribute to her surpassing beauty. They deplored the hold it gave her over her lover, however, blaming the malign influence of the Yang family for the disaster that overtook both Hsuan Tsung and his empire in A.D. 755.

Hsuan Tsung, who ruled from 713 to 756, was one of the great emperors of Chinese history; a shrewd, determined, and dynamic sovereign under whom the T'ang dynasty (see chart, page 20) reached the high noon of its territorial expansion and cultural brilliance. Gibbon's famous description of second-century Rome, "The fairest part of the earth, and the most civilized portion of mankind," summed up the Chinese empire in the first half of the eighth century with even greater aptness. In less than a hundred years, the T'ang emperors had recovered lands lost for five centuries. In the far west, Hsuan Tsung's empire stretched across the Tarim basin (see map, page 28), and Chinese suzerainty was acknowledged in Tibet and beyond the Pamirs (where Tashkent, Bukhara, and Samarkand were protected by Chinese arms and allied with China against the advancing Arabs). To the northeast, Hsuan Tsung controlled part of Manchuria and exercised suzerainty

over Korea, united for the first time. To the south, his empire reached into the Indo-Chinese peninsula.

At the center of these far-flung territories, in northwestern China on the site of modern Sian, stood Hsuan Tsung's main capital, Ch'ang-an or "Perpetual Peace," one of the most cultured and cosmopolitan cities of its time. A million residents lived within the twenty-two miles of perimeter wall; with another million people living outside, this was probably the largest conurbation the world had ever seen. Yet the city was meticulously planned, laid out like a chessboard and aligned on the cardinal points of the compass like the major capitals elsewhere in Asia. According to the American T'ang scholar Edward H. Shafer, the eleven major north-south avenues were each more than 482 feet wide, and even the narrowest of the fourteen east-west avenues was 226 feet wide. The imposing nature of these thoroughfares, which were flanked by trees, drainage ditches, and footpaths, is further emphasized by Shafer's revealing comparison of them with New York's Fifth Avenue, which is only one hundred feet wide.

To the capital of Ch'ang-an, across the East China Sea and along the central Asian silk route, came traders and travelers, envoys and students, to marvel at the great city and its glittering court. The impressed Japanese modeled two successive imperial capitals — Nara and Kyoto — on Ch'ang-an's chessboard pattern. They also transplanted Chinese legal, administrative, and fiscal practices to their island nation, adapted various forms of Chinese Buddhism, and adopted the Chinese language for official and scholarly use. With the Chinese language came the poetry that was the greatest glory of the T'ang dynasty's resplendent culture.

In poetry, Hsuan Tsung's reign represented the apex of T'ang achievement, and it is through the sharply critical eyes of the great poet Tu Fu that one catches a glimpse of the extravagance of the court and the arrogance of Yang Kuei-fei's family, all of whom had risen with her. These included her sisters, whom she had managed to have ennobled, and her brother Yang Kuo-chung, who became the emperor's prime minister. In "Ballad of the Beautiful Ladies," Tu Fu describes a palace picnic in April 753, only two years before the great An Lu-shan Rebellion, which was to topple Emperor Hsuan Tsung and cause the violent death of Yang Kuei-fei:

> . . . by the winding stream at Ch'ang-an
> Lovely ladies walk, looking
> Proudly ahead, then exchanging
> Sweet and charming smiles with
> Each other; faces so beautiful,
> Perfect figures showing through silk
> Draperies embroidered with
> Golden peacocks or silver unicorns;
> Their heads dressed in kingfisher
> Colours, with hanging pendants of
> Cut jade; on their backs little
> Over-garments studded with pearls;
> Amongst this galaxy the sisters
> Of Yang Kuei-fei, bearing great titles;
> Dishes served include the purple meat
> Of camel's hump, white slices of raw
> Fish on crystal plates; yet these
> Hardly satisfied jaded taste; all that
> Has taken so much thought and work
> To prepare, left hardly touched . . .

> Important guests and their retinues
> Crowd in; at last comes the greatest,
> Nonchalantly, on his horse . . .
> Prime Minister Yang is all powerful,
> His slightest touch will burn;
> Best to keep clear of him and his
> Evil temper.

Yang Kuei-fei had married one of Hsuan Tsung's sons in 736 when she was eighteen. As the legal wife of a prince, she was presented to the emperor on the day following her wedding. Quite possibly Hsuan Tsung, already fifty-one, was smitten by her then, but it was not until some time later that he was prepared to face the scandal of purloining his son's wife. In 741, Yang Kuei-fei repudiated her marriage vows to enter a Taoist nunnery, and she and the emperor probably became secret lovers at that time. In 745, Hsuan Tsung formally conferred the title of "Precious Consort" upon Yang Kuei-fei, and at the same time arranged to have his son married to another woman. Hsuan Tsung, who had ruled the empire conscientiously for thirty-two years, began to neglect his imperial duties. He abandoned his early audiences and, fortified by aphrodisiacs, dallied in bed with Yang Kuei-fei, who is described by her biographer Howard Levy as a "full-bosomed voluptuary." Music, dancing, and feasting became the major preoccupations of the court and its ruler.

In their revelries, Hsuan Tsung and Yang Kuei-fei reserved a special place for General An Lu-shan whenever he visited Ch'ang-an. An Lu-shan personified the cosmopolitan nature of the T'ang court. His father had been a Sogdian from Bukhara, his mother Turkish, but despite his non-Chinese origins, he had risen to be-

At the height of his power, T'ang dynasty emperor
Hsuan Tsung presided over a sprawling empire, a
cosmopolitan capital, and a glittering court — all
of which he sacrificed in his heedless passion for
Yang Kuei-fei. Enslaved by the charms of "Precious
Consort" Yang, Hsuan Tsung abandoned statecraft
for dalliance — and his empire drifted into anarchy.
In A.D. 755 one of the emperor's trusted field
commanders led a rebel force against the capital,
bringing both reign and romance to a tragic close.
At right, the feckless emperor is shown conversing
with his black-clad son. Below, Yang Kuei-fei's
handmaidens help her mount a horse.

come one of Hsuan Tsung's principal commanders in the defense of the T'ang frontiers against foreign "barbarians." His headquarters were at Yuchow, the site of modern Peking. On his trips to the capital, An Lu-shan, a man of great corpulence, assumed the role of court buffoon. On his forty-eighth birthday in 751 — at his own request — Yang Kuei-fei adopted him as her son, and a few days later the obese general was wrapped in swaddling clothes and given the ceremonial washing of the newborn child by Yang Kuei-fei and her ladies-in-waiting. It is said that the emperor was amused, presumably scorning the rumors that his favorite had become the general's mistress as well as mother.

While the court played, the country was visited with an ominous crescendo of calamities. In the spring of 750 there was a drought of great severity, and the emperor was forced to cancel a costly pilgrimage to a sacred mountain. In the spring of 751, the grain fleet went up in flames en route to Ch'ang-an and some two hundred ships were lost. In the very same month, another fire destroyed half a million weapons in the capital's main arsenal. In the summer, the empire suffered two great military defeats at the hands of the barbarians, one in South China and one in the northwest. In the autumn, endless rains brought great floods; the damage to Ch'ang-an was particularly serious. In the summer of 752, it was the eastern capital, Loyang, that suffered — this time from a great hurricane. In the fall of 753 there were more floods; grain prices shot up and the government had to release its reserves at reduced prices. In the autumn of 754, it was the same story: two months of rain, immense flood damage at both capitals, and rising grain prices, which the government

vainly attempted to control by selling its own stores at artificially low prices. Tu Fu, whose own son died of hunger a few weeks before the rebellion began in 755, expressed some of the widespread popular anger directed at the self-indulgent emperor and his court in an explosion of personal grief:

> . . . but while
> There comes the reek of wines
> And meats that rot inside the gates
> Of these rich, the bones of the
> Starving and cold are strewn along
> The roadsides . . .

The agent of retribution was not a tribune of the people, however, but a member of the innermost court circle, a man distinguished from his fellows only by the great military strength at his command. Of course, An Lu-shan's popularity and power had not pleased all the members of the Yang family, and when Yang Kuo-chung became prime minister in 752 he set about to discredit the general, whom he clearly regarded as a dangerous rival. While Yang was unable to build up an army equal to that of An Lu-shan, who controlled half the troops of the empire, he was sufficiently successful in undermining the general's position at court for the latter to decide to resort to force.

In December 755, An Lu-shan broke into open revolt and marched upon the imperial forces. Early in 756, he proclaimed himself the founder of a new dynasty, the Great Yen, after the ancient name for the Peking region. An Lu-shan met only weak resistance, and when, in July 756, his army seized the strategic pass leading from the North China plain to Ch'ang-an, the emperor Hsuan Tsung, Yang Kuei-fei, and Yang Kuo-chung

The T'ang capital of Ch'ang-an was a vast atelier, supporting sculptors, goldsmiths, and painters as well as poets and historians. During Hsuan Tsung's reign, skilled artisans flocked to the imperial palace — a warren of small, gabled pavilions and interconnecting courtyards much like the one seen in the fourteenth-century scroll shown at right. T'ang craftsmen remain largely anonymous, but their delicately wrought and elegantly finished works reflect the urbane splendor of their capital as faithfully as do the lapidary verses of Li Po and Tu Fu, the dynasty's preeminent poets. Under one such artist's hand, for example, the ungainly bulk of the camel is transformed into an object of supple line and vibrant hue (below). The brace of Buddhist angels above, the work of another T'ang craftsman, seems to have been spun out of gold filament.

DYNASTIES OF CHINA

Chinese history has been punctuated by periods of civil chaos, military insurrection, and political anarchy, but for simplicity's sake those interregnums have been deleted from the dynasty chart below. Also missing are the names of a number of small, regional governments that ruled concurrently with a major dynasty. The exception to this rule occurs during the Sung period, when two vigorous and independent dynasties — the Liao and the Chin — controlled North China.

SHANG (c. 1766–1122 B.C.)

CHOU (1122–256 B.C.)
   City of Chi built on site of modern Peking
   Age of Confucius

CH'IN (221–207 B.C.)
   Shih Huang Ti, first emperor of united China
   Great Wall completed

HAN (206 B.C.–A.D. 220)

WEI (A.D. 220–264)

CHIN (265–419)

SUI (589–618)
   Grand Canal completed

T'ANG (618–906)
   Cultural renaissance under Hsuan Tsung (713–756)
   An Lu-shan Rebellion (755)

LIAO (907–1125)
   Khitan establish southern capital at Peking

SUNG (960–1279)

CHIN (1115–1234)
   First imperial palaces constructed at Peking
   Genghis Khan captures city

YÜAN (1260–1368)
   Kublai Khan rebuilds capital
   Mongols rule all China from Peking

MING (1368–1644)
   Yüan Great Interior leveled by Hung Wu
      (1368–98)
   Forbidden City rebuilt by Yung Lo (1403–24)

CH'ING (1644–1912)
   K'ang-hsi (1661–1722), greatest Manchu emperor
   Under Ch'ien Lung (1736–95), dynasty reaches
      apogee
   Opium War (1839–42)
   Taiping Rebellion (1850–64)
   Boxer Rebellion (1900)
   Death of Empress Dowager Tz'u Hsi (1908)

fled the capital by night. On their flight toward Szechwan in the southwest, their troops mutinied, killed Yang Kuo-chung, and forced the emperor to have Yang Kuei-fei strangled. Shortly afterwards the heartbroken Hsuan Tsung abdicated in favor of the crown prince.

As the famous romance reached its tragic climax, An Lu-shan's army captured Ch'ang-an. Members of the royal family and those connected with the aristocracy and officialdom were executed in horrible ways, and the treasures of the capital were seized and dispatched to An Lu-shan's headquarters at Yuchow. One can understand why an eighteenth-century Chinese scholar has called the An Lu-shan Rebellion a sign that the "imperial aura" of Ch'ang-an was shifting to Peking. But that observation was written with the benefit of a thousand years of hindsight; it could not have looked that way at the time. The Great Yen dynasty itself did not last long: An Lu-shan was soon killed by his son, who was in turn assassinated by another rebel leader, who was slain by *his* son. With the ebb and flow of rebellion and foreign invasion over the next decade, Ch'ang-an changed hands repeatedly, and finally the T'ang returned.

The old aristocracy of the Ch'ang-an region had been decimated. As Tu Fu observed:
   Well said Ch'ang-an looks like a chess-board:
   A hundred years of the saddest news.
   The mansions of princes and nobles all have new lords:
   Another breed is capped and robed for office.
But the disappearance of the old aristocracy did not seem to diminish Ch'ang-an's importance. In fact, the position of the aristocracy had been seriously undermined even before the An Lu-shan Rebellion by the rise of the new meritocracy of T'ang civil servants. Hsuan

The sinewy grace and awesome countenance of the T'ang lion at left reflect both the elegance and the strength of the dynasty in its golden years. Like the lion, T'ang emperors of the early eighth century ruled virtually without challenge in their domain. By mid-century, however, licentiousness had corroded that elegance and misrule had eroded that strength. Like the Ch'in long before them, the T'ang were forced to yield to a new dynasty.
Overleaf:
In the vacuum created by the collapse of the Ch'in dynasty (see chart opposite), civil war was almost inevitable. Rival claimants dueled for four years before one, Liu Pang, was able to proclaim victory. A scroll detail recreates his triumphal entry into the liberated imperial capital.

Tsung and his predecessors had perfected the system, initiated by the Han dynasty seven centuries earlier, of recruiting ministers and administrators by examination. Thus, China had created the first truly modern civil service — an innovation that was not copied in the West until another millennium had passed. It was the existence of this great bureaucracy that permitted the T'ang dynasty to quickly resume the functions of government once order had been reimposed.

The capital of China was once again the center of the greatest empire in the world, and it continued to impress foreign visitors. The Ch'ang-an region in the valley of the Wei River had been the site of the capitals of China's greatest dynasties for the previous two thousand years; there seemed to be no reason why it should not continue in that role. Its advantages had been summed up in verse by a famous Chinese historian of the first century A.D.:

> In abundance of flowering plants and fruits
> it is the most fertile of the Nine Provinces
> In natural barriers for protection and defense
> it is the most impregnable refuge in heaven
>   and earth
> This is why its influence has extended in six
> directions
> This is why it has thrice become the seat of
> imperial power.

It was the strategic location of the Wei valley — easily defensible, but with access through the gorges of the Yellow River to the fertile land of North China — that had enabled the Chou dynasty to use it as a springboard to conquer the Shang dynasty cities of the plain and set up a loose-knit, feudal empire. After centuries of rule, the weakened Chou dynasty was forced by barbarian pressure from the west to move permanently to its secondary capital at Loyang. The Ch'in, who displaced the Chou in the Wei valley, emulated the previous dynasty by conquering the rest of the country from that powerful base. By uniting the feudal states that had emerged as the Chou grip slackened, they created the first centralized Chinese empire in 221 B.C.

The Ch'in dynasty was extremely short-lived, but its swift demise was due to the oppressive reign of its founder, Shih Huang Ti, and not to the declining importance of the Wei valley. Indeed, the Ch'in had increased the strength of the area by a massive irrigation scheme that had greatly increased the region's agricultural output — and Liu Pang, the peasant who founded the renowned Han dynasty, emerged victorious from the post-Ch'in civil war largely because he controlled the Wei valley. He built the first Ch'ang-an near the site of the former Ch'in capital.

As the Han empire began to prosper, the appetite of its capital grew, exceeding the agricultural resources of even the Wei valley. The produce of the "most fertile of the Nine Provinces" was no longer enough. Ch'ang-an became a parasite, fattening upon the grain surpluses of more fruitful areas. In Han times, this meant the North China plain — as the increasing attention paid by the dynasty to flood control measures along the Yellow River shows. Sometime after A.D. 25, the dynasty, weakened by the interregnum of a usurper, moved permanently to the eastern capital of Loyang. Situated within the economic area upon which it had come to depend, this second Han dynasty became known as the Eastern, or Later, Han.

But Ch'ang-an was far from finished. It became the capital again when the city's continuing strategic merits were demonstrated in the sixth century. After the collapse of the Later Han dynasty, ties between North and South China were severed, and both regions became battlegrounds for contending dynasties that divided and subdivided the two areas in bewildering succession. Finally, a dynasty based in the Wei valley emulated the Chou and the Ch'in by sallying forth across the North China plain and reuniting the entire region. In 589, after usurping the throne and founding the Sui dynasty, Sui Wen Ti conquered the south and recreated the Ch'in-Han empire after more than 350 years of disunity. Sui Wen Ti kept his capital in the Wei valley, an area sanctified by its historic associations with the Sui dynasty's great predecessors. Using ancient methods of divination, his geomancers chose a new site, southeast of the old Han capital, for the dynasty's capital. At an astrologically auspicious time, work was begun on the vast metropolis that would become, after the overthrow of the Sui, the great T'ang capital of Ch'ang-an.

The China reunited under the Sui and T'ang dynasties was economically very different from the empire ruled by the Han. During the centuries of disunity, the incursions of barbarians into northern China had driven many Chinese south into the Lower Yangtze valley. The newly settled lands were cleared of swamp and jungle and made suitable for agriculture by the construction of dams, reservoirs, and irrigation canals. By the time the Sui came to power, the Yangtze valley had outstripped the North China plain in economic strength.

The importance of the Lower Yangtze valley to the Sui empire in general and to Ch'ang-an in particular was immediately appreciated by Sui Wen Ti. The result of his perception was the construction of the Grand Canal, which was designed to facilitate the dispatch of tax grain to the capital city. The canal, another example of the ruthless determination of rulers and the patient endurance of the masses that dominates the history of China, had an immediate and profound impact upon the country. Within the course of a quarter of a century, Sui Wen Ti and his son Sui Yang Ti built, improved, extended, or linked up some one thousand miles of waterway stretching in four main sections from Hangchow, south of the Yangtze, to Ch'ang-an. In his edict ordering the construction of the final section of the canal — from Loyang, again the subsidiary capital, to Ch'ang-an — Sui Yang Ti justified the immense hardships that he was about to impose upon his subjects:

. . . starting from T'ungkuan in the east and leading the water of the Wei from the west, a canal should be cut by human effort. The work is easy and can be accomplished. Artisans and workers have already looked over the site at my order. Adapting the canal to geographical conditions and considering the meaning [and requirements] of permanence, once the canal is cut, it will not be destroyed for ten thousand generations. It will enable the government and private persons to navigate big boats, and from dawn to dusk, grain tribute can be transported ceaselessly upstream and downstream. [Thus] the work of several tens of days would save hundreds of millions. I know that in the hot summer, work easily brings fatigue; but with-

From time immemorial China's inland capitals have been dependent upon a fragile system of waterways and canals, their lifeline to the Yangtze valley rice bowl. Amply supplied with grain, these imperial cities flourished; cut off, they languished and eventually collapsed. The cultivation, transportation, and storage of rice therefore became a national concern, one reflected in such T'ang tomb pottery as the bullock cart above and the granary jar below. So critical was the maintenance of this link with the south that the Han, whose ties with a more nomadic past are evidenced by the tomb figure of a sheepcote at left above, built watchtowers along the route. A pottery model of one such lookout is seen at right.

The Yangtze valley cornucopia was coveted by rival warlords throughout China's imperial era, and consequently the nation's history is one of incessant internecine strife. Even the Han, who held the Yangtze valley for more than four centuries, did so only at the price of constant vigilance. The tranquil scene at right, a Sung artist's recreation of life at the Han palace, belies the bellicose nature of the inhabitants, whose expansionist rule was one of the most dynamic in Chinese annals. Hu piao *like* the one at right, below, were used by the Han to verify the authenticity of their communiqués with the front. One half accompanied the commander into battle, the other was enclosed in the orders he received from the palace. If the halves fit, the message was acted upon. Heavily armed cavalry (left) then rode forth under the protection of the Han god of war (above).

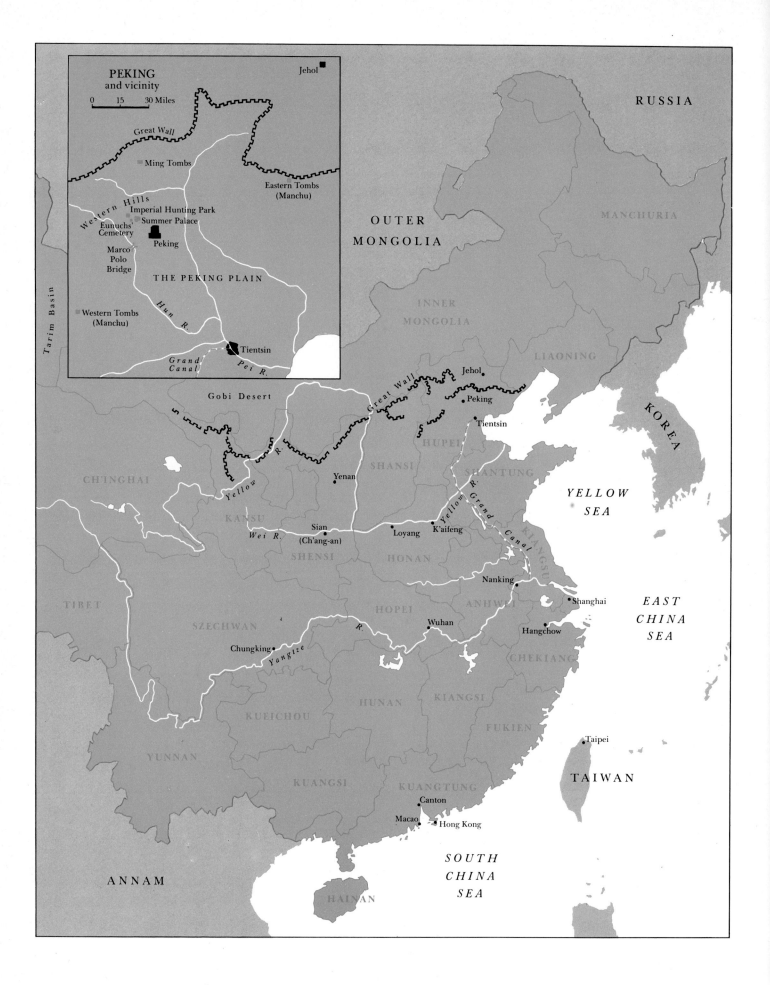

PEKING
and vicinity

0   15   30 Miles

Jehol

Great Wall

Ming Tombs

Eastern Tombs
(Manchu)

Western Hills

Imperial Hunting Park
Summer Palace

Eunuchs'
Cemetery

Peking

Marco
Polo
Bridge

THE PEKING PLAIN

Tarim Basin

Western Tombs
(Manchu)

Hun R.

Grand
Canal

Pei R.

Tientsin

RUSSIA

OUTER
MONGOLIA

MANCHURIA

INNER
MONGOLIA

LIAONING

Gobi Desert

Great Wall

Jehol

Peking

Tientsin

KOREA

HUPEI

CH'INGHAI

Yellow R.

SHANSI

Yenan

SHANTUNG

Yellow R.

Grand Canal

YELLOW
SEA

KANSU

Wei R.

Sian
(Ch'ang-an)

Loyang

K'aifeng

SHENSI

HONAN

KIANGSU

Nanking

Shanghai

EAST
CHINA
SEA

TIBET

HOPEI

R.

Wuhan

Hangchow

SZECHWAN

Yangtze

ANHWEI

Chungking

CHEKIANG

HUNAN

KIANGSI

KUEICHOU

FUKIEN

YUNNAN

Taipei

TAIWAN

KUANGSI

KUANGTUNG

Canton

Macao

Hong Kong

ANNAM

HAINAN

SOUTH
CHINA
SEA

The development of long stirrups — which gave the rider a much steadier seat on his mount when riding at a full gallop — made the T'ang cavalry a formidable military force. The new saddle is featured on the bas-relief panel at left, which decorated the Shensi tomb of a T'ang emperor. From their capital at Ch'ang-an (modern Sian), T'ang horsemen extended their suzerainty over the whole of central China and much of Manchuria and Sinkiang (west of the Gobi Desert).

out temporary labour, how could permanent rest be made possible?

By the time this final section of the canal was built, the subjects of the Sui were well aware that the project would entail rather more than a little extra exertion in the midday sun. According to an eighteenth-century Chinese account, over 3,500,000 workers between the ages of fifteen and fifty had been conscripted for the longest section; attempts to escape were punishable by decapitation. Each family was required to contribute one person — a child, an old man, or a woman — to help prepare meals for the workers, and some 50,000 "young and brave" soldiers armed with sticks were employed to keep order. With administrators added in, the total work force was estimated at almost 5,500,000 people. In addition to constructing the one-hundred-foot-wide canal, these workers were responsible for building roads and planting trees along each bank. The result was that the shadows of elms and willows overlapped along more than 650 miles of the canal. In addition, between Ch'ang-an and the Yangtze, some forty palaces were constructed along the canal for the convenience of the emperor.

By the time the project was finished, 2,500,000 workers are said to have perished, along with 23,000 soldiers. The figures may be exaggerated, but they do give an idea of the immensity of the endeavor and the harshness of the working conditions. The Grand Canal was a great feat of medieval civil engineering, but even at a distance of 1,300 years it is difficult to forget the appalling human cost. As a later Chinese historian wrote, Sui Yang Ti "shortened the life of his dynasty by a number of years but benefited posterity to ten

thousand generations. He ruled without benevolence, but his rule is to be credited with enduring accomplishments." Within a decade of the completion of the Grand Canal, the tyrannical Sui Yang Ti had been assassinated and the Sui dynasty had been succeeded by the T'ang.

The water route that the T'ang were fortunate enough to inherit did much to make Ch'ang-an viable. Transporting the grain from the Yangtze still took roughly a year, however, because when one section of the Grand Canal was usable, the next would be dried up or in flood. Ships might be delayed for as long as three months at some points, and much pilfering took place. The inefficiency meant that when the Ch'ang-an region had a bad harvest, the T'ang emperors had to move to their subsidiary capital at Loyang, nearer to the Yangtze rice bowl. Under Hsuan Tsung, leading officials finally solved this perennial problem by establishing large granaries at important junctions of the Grand Canal. When one section of the canal proved impassable, the grain was stored and the boats returned to their port of origin; other boats were hired locally to take the grain on to the T'ang capital as soon as conditions permitted.

So successful was this scheme that by the end of the eighth century the Lower Yangtze provinces were providing nine-tenths of the country's total land tax, although their population still represented only a quarter of the country's total. Annual grain shipments from the south to the capital rose as much as one thousand per cent by the middle of the T'ang. To ensure the stability of these supplies, the T'ang gradually concentrated more and more of their water conservation activ-

The Sui, who succeeded the Han in 589, devoted their brief and repressive reign to constructing the Grand Canal. The one-thousand-mile canal, aorta of the grain shipment route, was finished in less than a quarter of a century — at a cost of 2,600 lives per mile. Sumptuous palaces lined its banks, elms and willows overarched its waters, and dragon boats such as the one pictured at right plied its hundred-foot-wide channels. Today the barges and the palaces are gone (below), but much of the canal is as navigable as it was almost 1,400 years ago.

ities in the fertile provinces of the Lower Yangtze.

But the maintenance of a capital a thousand miles from its economic base, however efficient the transportation system, required a strong dynasty that could protect its lines of communication. Both the Chou and the Han, when weakened, had moved their capital eastward to Loyang — and closer to their economic base. The T'ang managed to stay at Ch'ang-an after the body blow of the An Lu-shan Rebellion, but their successors, the Sung, who reunited the empire fifty years after the fall of the T'ang, were weak from the start. They never controlled the sixteen prefectures around the Peking area, and they were eventually forced out of northern China altogether. Recognizing economic and political realities, they had chosen Kaifeng, which lay even farther east than Loyang and three hundred miles nearer the southern rice bowl than Ch'ang-an, as their first capital. After evacuating northern China around the year 1127, the Later, or Southern, Sung dynasty shifted the capital to Hangchow, the southern terminus of the Grand Canal, in 1135. Since this was where the grain ships were loaded when supplies had to be sent to a northern capital, the new seat of government symbolized the unification of the political and economic centers of China. To all intents and purposes, the impact of the An Lu-shan Rebellion had been to shift the imperial aura from the Wei valley southward to the Yangtze valley, not northward from Ch'ang-an to Peking. There seemed to be no good reason why an imperial capital should ever occupy the site of Peking. Yet the imperial history of Peking began within twenty years of the establishment of the Southern Sung capital at Hangchow.

II

Behind the Great Wall

The remains of Peking man, discovered twenty-six miles southwest of the city in 1929, are proof that the area was inhabited as far back as half a million years ago. In early historic times, however, the Peking region stood on the fringe of Chinese civilization. The small Peking plain is situated in the northwest corner of the North China plain and is ringed by mountains to the west, northwest, and north (see map, page 28). To the northwest, a pass opens onto the Mongolian plateau; to the north, another pass leads to the mountains of the northeast. Moving eastward along the southern edge of those mountains, one reaches the coastal pass, Shanhaikuan, that leads into Manchuria. The Peking plain was thus a natural junction between plateau and plain, but in ancient times access was restricted by the marshes to the south and southeast. To enter from the North China plain, one had to come from the southwest, passing between mountains and marsh and crossing the Yungting River at a ford which, millennia later, was the site of what Europeans came to call the Marco Polo Bridge. The Yungting River was subject to unpredictable flooding, and for that reason the site of the first settlement was located some seven miles to the northeast of the ford. Here a town called Chi was to grow up.

The story goes that when the Chou dynasty overthrew the Shang, they settled the descendants of the legendary Yellow Emperor at Chi to rule a small fief. Recent scholarship indicates that the fief, known as Yen, was actually bestowed upon the Duke of Shao, one of the two highest officials in the court of the first Chou king. The duke, busy at court, entrusted this remote territory to his eldest son. It was an important respon-

sibility, for the fief had probably been established as the first line of defense against the non-Chinese barbarians to the north.

It must be understood that the distinction between Chinese and barbarian was not racial. Two great Chinese dynasties, the Chou and the Ch'in, are thought to have been barbarian in origin and Chinese by assimilation. Hsuan Tsung had Turkish blood, and his ancestors founded the T'ang dynasty with the help of Turkish cavalry. The real cleavage between the two was a cultural one, fostered by climate. To be Chinese meant to be a farmer. Yellow loess dust, brought from the northwest by the wind and by the powerful waters of the Yellow River, had made the North China plain highly fertile. Intensive cultivation produced an agricultural surplus, which permitted the growth of a sophisticated culture. To the north, geography prevented this. Rainfall in that region is irregular and sparse; the rivers are pitiful streams compared with the great Yellow River and the Yangtze; oases exist, but they are isolated from each other by vast stretches of desert. With the exception of a few areas, the shortage of water prevents intensive agriculture in the Chinese manner. Man survives, but in small numbers and mainly by raising livestock and hunting. Ever moving between summer and winter pastures, the steppe nomad was contemptuous of the Chinese peasant, who was tied to his plot of yellow earth. But every so often the riches and the fruitfulness of the plain tempted a tribe to abandon its nomadic frugality, and fierce cavalry would descend upon the Chinese empire.

The ever-present threat of nomad raids made China's climatic and cultural frontier a military frontier as

well. After the Chou empire began to split up into warring states in the fifth century B.C., succeeding kingdoms on the frontier began to build walls along their northern boundaries as a defense against barbarian attack. These walls were later utilized by the first Ch'in emperor when he built the Great Wall, the most tangible mark of a rift between civilizations to be found anywhere in the world. It was a symbolic barrier as well, for the Ch'in extended the wall into mountainous areas where no nomad cavalry could ever tread — but where the wall could still protect the Middle Kingdom (the meaning of the Chinese word for China) from the nameless demons of the north.

The Great Wall (overleaf) could not prevent all contact between the two peoples, of course. In the hills on the edge of the plain there was a sort of climatic no-man's-land where Chinese agriculture and barbarian pastoralism could be practiced side by side. The existence of these marginal lands meant that the frontier areas were more exposed to non-Chinese customs and ideas — and therefore more receptive to what other Chinese might regard as outlandish ideologies.

During the tremendous intellectual ferment that accompanied the Warring States period — a ferment matched only by Periclean Athens — each state tended to favor one or two of the contending one hundred schools. A certain provincial naïveté, a greater simplicity of outlook — or perhaps just the influence of barbarian superstitions — led the rulers of Yen to espouse the doctrines of *yin* and *yang* and the Five Elements School.

Proponents of the doctrine of *yin* and *yang* argued that the universe encompassed an extraordinary dualism of forces: the *yin*, negative, feminine, darkness,

cold, wetness, passivity; and the *yang*, positive, masculine, light, warmth, dryness, activity. Significantly, the *yin* and the *yang* were complementary, unlike the Persians' antagonistic dualism of good and evil, which was absorbed into Christianity. The Five Elements School held that earth, wood, metal, fire, and water were not so much physical substances as prime natural forces, always following each other in an ever-recurring cycle. Thus these elements alternated in dominance during the course of the year and over the years and controlled both natural and human events, which were thus intertwined. Each dynasty had its element, and each ruler was supposed to decide his place of residence, the color of his clothes, his choice of food, and the acts of his administration according to the season and its dominant element.

The doctrines of the five elements and *yin* and *yang* may have originated in magical practices, but the Chinese found the view of a universe based on harmony highly satisfying intellectually — so much so that they eventually incorporated it into orthodox Confucianism. An offshoot of the theories of *yin* and *yang* and the five elements was *feng-shui* ("wind-water"), or geomancy — the art of "adapting residences of the living and the dead so as to cooperate and harmonize with the local currents of the cosmic breath." Geomancy played a major role in the siting of both Ch'ang-an and Peking.

By the time of the Warring States period, the state of Yen had spread beyond the small plain that encircled its capital and into the southern portion of Manchuria. By this route, the doctrine of *yin-yang* reached the Korean peninsula — where today the symbols for *yin*

and *yang* occupy the center of the flag of South Korea. From Korea, the doctrine was carried to Japan — where, in the eighth century, the Bureau of *Yin* and *Yang* studied natural phenomena to help in formulating official policy.

The doctrines of *yin* and *yang* and the five elements were to prove influential and enduring, but the state of Yen itself disappeared in 222 B.C., incorporated into the empire of the Wei valley state of Ch'in. Chi lost its status as a capital and became merely a provincial city for the next four centuries. During the 350 years of disunity that followed the collapse of the Han dynasty in A.D. 220, the name of Yen was once more heard in the land; the barbarians who conquered the northern section of the Yellow River plain named their ephemeral regimes after the ancient state. Under the T'ang, the area once more reverted to provincial status and the city of Chi was renamed Yuchow. Subsequently, Yuchow grew in importance as defense against the barbarians became a crucial concern of successive T'ang governments. It was the continual strengthening of this frontier command that, as we have seen, provided An Lu-shan with the army with which he attempted to set up his Great Yen dynasty.

With the fall of the T'ang in 907 and the advent of another, shorter period of disunity, the status of the Peking area underwent a decisive change. A short-lived successor to the T'ang dynasty awarded the sixteen prefectures of the region to a Mongol people called the Khitan (or Khitai, from which the English word "Cathay" is derived). The Khitan homeland was in the mountains north of the Peking area, but southern Manchuria was also under Khitan control. With a portion of the North China plain in their possession, the Khitan rulers set themselves up as a Chinese dynasty under the name of Liao. Even a China reunited under the Sung in 960 proved unable to wrest the sixteen prefectures from the Liao, who had made Yuchow their southern capital. In 936 they had renamed the ancient city Nanking, or "Southern Capital." It was also known as Yenching ("Yen Capital"), a name which has persisted as a literary name for Peking.

The Peking area, having long been a melting pot of Chinese and alien ideas, now became a laboratory for the creation of a hybrid-Chinese barbarian political institution. This was the beginning of more than four centuries of gradually increasing barbarian control of China — a period that culminated in the rule of the entire country for the first time by a completely alien dynasty, the Mongol Yüan. It was also the beginning of the rise of Peking to the status of imperial capital.

It was an inauspicious start. The newly christened southern capital was only one of five Liao capitals: there was also a central, a western, and an eastern capital, in addition to a supreme capital in the heart of the Khitan homeland. The supreme capital was specifically designed as a Chinese walled city, but very little was done to give the southern capital a new look, apart from the construction of a very small Imperial City in the southwest corner. It is recorded, however, that in the three markets of the southern capital "all the products of the soil and the sea" could be obtained.

One reason for the failure to rebuild the southern capital may have been that the Liao emperors spent little time there. The Khitan engaged in some agriculture, but they were principally a pastoral people, meas-

uring their wealth in sheep and horses. The Liao rulers preserved the nomadic life-style of their people in their annual round of activities, spending each season in an appropriate part of their dominions. According to the official dynastic history:

> During the autumn and winter they shunned the cold; during the spring and summer they avoided the heat. Following water and grass and engaging in hunting and fishing made up the yearly routine. For each of the four seasons [the emperor] had a temporary place in which to reside. This was called a *na-po*.

A *na-po* appears to have been a large tented encampment, a veritable "felt city," according to one visiting Sung official. None of the four main seasonal *na-po* was located near the southern capital, though from time to time the emperors were to be found hunting duck and swans in the late spring at a large lake in its vicinity. Liao emperors engaged in hunting at this particular lake whenever they visited the southern capital. We hear of one emperor making a visit to Yen in 1025, a year when the region had had a particularly good harvest:

> The emperor paid his respects to the aged, showed his kindness to widowers and widows, and gave a banquet. The drinking lasted until nightfall. Six streets were lighted by lanterns as if it were daytime. Officials and commoners strolled about, enjoying themselves. The emperor also looked on incognito.

Relations were not always so cordial between the Liao emperors and their Chinese subjects. On one occasion a senior minister described the people of Yen as "tricky and cunning" and accused them of evading taxes and corvée labor. The emperor, who sent a senior official to admonish the miscreants, had good reason to be apprehensive about the Chinese population. Like all barbarian conquerors of Chinese territory, the Khitan emperors found themselves in an immensely inferior numerical position. The total population of the Liao empire was probably something under four million — of which only about 750,000, or one-fifth, were Khitan and at least 2,400,000, or nearly two-thirds, were Chinese. The remainder consisted of various other subject peoples. The danger of assimilation was clearly great, and the Liao emperors went to considerable lengths to preserve the distinctness of the Khitan culture. The great Khitan ruler A-peo-chi, who founded the Liao dynasty, knew Chinese but was reluctant to use it, fearing that his tribal followers would imitate him — a practice "which would make the soldiers timid and weak." Under A-peo-chi, two forms of script, one alphabetic and one based on modified Chinese characters, were invented for the Khitan language and used widely in government affairs, although Chinese remained the lingua franca of the empire.

This duality permeated other areas of contact between the two cultures. A-peo-chi stabilized the Liao imperial line by substituting the Chinese hereditary system for the Khitan custom of electing a ruler for a three-year term, but the Khitan tribal kinship system was preserved. Confucius was proclaimed the supreme sage of the state, but Confucianism failed to become a meaningful state ideology. Literary studies were respected among the Liao's Chinese subjects, but the Khitan scorned book learning. (This attitude may have affected the Liao's Chinese subjects as well, for the dynasty is notable for its failure to produce any sig-

Generations after they abandoned the steppes of Central Asia for a more settled life as overlords of North China, the Tatars retained a firm sense of their unique tribal tradition. As a result, Khitan and Mongol emperors alike spent the greater part of each year in restless migration from one subsidiary capital to another. These na-po, or "felt cities" — one of which is featured in the scroll detail below — were little more than vast tented encampments, throwbacks to the Tatars' nomadic past. The barbarians were horsemen of almost legendary skill, and even in their highly sedentary role as administrators of agrarian China they found time for riding. The scroll at right depicts a Mongol circus, an annual display of horsemanship.

nificant literary work in Chinese.) Chinese food was appreciated by the Liao rulers, but the Khitan continued to prefer the products of their herds, especially the fermented mare's milk called *koumiss*. Indeed, the two cultures remained so distinct that even after almost two hundred years of rule the Liao emperors did not realize that such dairy products were disliked intensely by Chinese inhabitants of the empire.

Some of the strongest indications of the persistence of Khitan tribal customs were displayed in the investiture of a new ruler, although the very purpose of that ceremony was to confer upon the Liao sovereign all the cachet of a truly Chinese emperor. First, a tribal ceremony of "rebirth" was performed in a special building. Welcomed at the entrance by his courtiers, each of whom held two bows, the future emperor entered and disrobed. Followed by a young boy, he walked three times under three V-shaped pieces of timber erected upside down inside the building. Each time he went under one of the arches, a midwife recited an incantation and stroked his body. When the boy had been under the arches seven times, the future ruler lay down by the timbers and an old man standing outside the building struck a quiver of arrows and shouted: "A boy is born." The chief priest then covered the future emperor's head, the courtiers congratulated him, and the midwife gave him some wine. Offered a choice of seven new names by seven old men, the new emperor selected the most auspicious one.

In a subsequent ceremony, the new emperor mounted a horse, galloped away, and fell off. The oldest men among his maternal relatives, acting as his grooms, then covered him with a felt rug. The use of the horse

in this ceremony is a clear indication of the ritual's origins in the inner Asian steppe. Even the final ceremony of the investiture, a Chinese-style ritual of "yielding," was performed on horseback. In this ceremony, the new emperor, seated on his favorite steed, sent a messenger to his senior officials and tribal leaders, who paid obeisance to him from a short distance. The message protested his unworthiness for the role of emperor, a self-deprecatory suggestion that his loyal followers of course denied.

The dual nature of the Liao empire was institutionalized in the division of the government into two halves, northern (Khitan) and southern (Chinese), each having its own officials and administrative apparatus, but both based in the supreme capital. The southern administration was modeled on the T'ang system, and some civil servants were even recruited through a version of the T'ang examination system. However, any Khitan who allowed his son to sit for the examinations was severely beaten, since the Khitan were expected to attain office by the traditional tribal system of hereditary privilege.

By and large, Khitan efforts to preserve themselves and their culture from submersion in that of the wealthier, more sophisticated, and larger Chinese population were successful. Chinese settlers were encouraged to cultivate suitable land in traditional Khitan territories, but the Khitan were never overwhelmed by this migration, as the Manchus later were. Indeed, the Chinese who contributed to the demise of the Liao dynasty were not subjects of that dynasty but of the Sung.

The Liao attempted to conquer the Sung empire, which controlled all of China to the south. For thirty long years they threw their well-disciplined, highly organized, and hard-hitting cavalry *ordos* (from which comes the English word "hordes") against the less mobile and less effective Sung armies. The Sung repelled them with a system of defense that relied heavily upon the use of fortresses and outposts along the frontier. They planted three million elm and willow trees along 750 miles of their common border with the northern Liao dynasty. They then dug canals and ditches, and constructed artificial lakes in this region; some of the watery cavalry traps were thirty miles long, fifteen miles wide, and ten feet deep. Behind these defenses, the well-fortified walled cities of the Sung empire were further obstacles, even after the Khitan developed effective siege-warfare techniques.

The Sung also buttressed their defenses with diplomacy, playing off the Hsi Hsia Tibetan kingdom on the Liao's western flank against their persistent attackers. Eventually, in 1004, the Liao emperors tired of their fruitless forays and allowed themselves to be bought off with costly tribute of silver and silk. It seemed like a great humiliation for the Sung; in fact it was the beginning of the decline of the Liao. If the Liao had conquered the Sung, they might have been able to establish a strong dynasty ruling all China. Instead, the Liao dream of world empire had been shattered, their sense of national purpose had been undermined, and their army, which had been preeminent for its mobility, stagnated behind a Maginot Line of forts and walled cities. According to their dynastic history, the Liao, "surrounded on the four sides by militant peoples, crouched in their midst like a tiger whom no one dared to challenge." But as peace softened the tiger's claws, as the

Following the collapse of the T'ang, China was carved up by lesser powers. Barbarians seized North China, but they were unable to dislodge the Sung dynasty from its capital at Kaifeng. Secure behind their "willow palisade" and fortified city walls, the Sung lived in hermetic splendor, heirs to the cultural tradition of the T'ang. In this serene atmosphere the decorative arts reached new heights — as evidenced by the burial crown at far left, a delicate corona of pearls, rubies, and gold florets. The Sung hair ornament at near left, a phoenix wrought of plaited and soldered gold wire, was created for the exclusive use of the empress. The bustling capital of the Sung dynasty is the subject of a famous scroll, Life Along the River on the Eve of Ch'ing Ming Festival. The panel below focuses upon an arched causeway on the city's outskirts.

Shrewd diplomacy and stout city walls gave the Sung a double line of defense against invasion, and for years the massive, tapering gates of Kaifeng (right) barred aggressors from the interior. The details seen above are all taken from another version of the Ch'ing Ming Festival scroll. Above left: a caravan of Bactrian camels passes in front of a wine-shop whose rich clientele are arriving in sedan chairs. Center: shallow-draft houseboats line the banks of the Pien Canal, the Sung capital's pipeline for produce. Right: tourists bound for the festival crowd the rails of a modest bridge that spans the city's moat.

fighting spirit of the Khitan *ordos* was eroded by lack of combat, a challenger did appear. The moment of truth occurred during an imperial fishing expedition.

In 1112, the man destined to be the last emperor of the Liao dynasty went to his spring *na-po* at Duck River Lake in northern Manchuria. The great felt city was pitched beside groves of elm, willow, and apricot trees on the sandy tracts near the lake. While the emperor was in residence, tributary Jurchen chieftains came from beyond the distant borders of the Liao empire for their customary audience. A great First Fish feast was given, and when everyone had drunk deeply the emperor, no better off than the rest, mounted his chariot decorated with dragons and, as was his right, ordered each of the Jurchen chieftains in turn to dance for him. Only one refused to perform this symbolic tribute of vassal to master. Standing erect and looking directly at the emperor, he refused on the grounds of inability and maintained his defiance in the face of repeated orders from the drunken Liao sovereign. The chieftain's name was A-ku-ta, and within ten years of the dramatic confrontation at Duck River Lake he had united the Jurchen tribes, overthrown the Liao, and set up the Chin empire.

The Jurchen victory was facilitated by an alliance with the Sung, who again adopted the old Chinese strategy of pitting one barbarian tribe against another in the hope of seeing their long-time foe, the Liao, finally vanquished. But A-ku-ta's successor proved ungrateful and began to make demands of the Sung that exceeded even those of the Liao. The Sung emperor Hui Tsung, a famous painter and patron of the arts, abdicated in despair and fled from Kaifeng just before a Chin army captured the Sung capital in 1125. In a second attack, both Hui Tsung and his successor were captured and carried off. The Sung soon rallied under a new emperor, Hui Tsung's son, and though the Chin armies crossed the Yangtze several times, the border between the Chin and Sung empires was finally stabilized along the Huai River, north of the Yangtze and roughly marking the northern limit of rice cultivation.

It was at this time that the Southern Sung moved their capital to Hangchow. The Chin, imitating their Liao predecessors, set up five capitals, but unlike the Liao they eventually made Yenching their main capital, renaming it Chung-tu ("Central Capital") in 1153. In a sense it was a logical move. An earlier barbarian dynasty, the Northern Wei, which had ruled the same portion of North China, had eventually moved its capital to the plain. For the Chin, who controlled Manchuria as well as the North China plain, Yenching was situated in a truly central position. Moreover, the Chin felt a far greater affinity for the Chinese way of life than the Khitan ever had, a factor that also influenced their decision. The Khitan had been primarily herdsmen with a marginal interest in agriculture; the Jurchen also had their herds, but in their less arid homeland they had been more dependent on agriculture, hunting, and fishing. They were readier to accept close contact with a society based on intensive agriculture.

Not that the Chin did not copy the Liao in taking measures to preserve the distinctiveness of the Jurchen culture and to prevent its complete assimilation by the Chinese. They adopted the Khitan alphabetic script for their language and later devised their own scripts, which were used with Chinese in government docu-

Hui Tsung, the penultimate emperor of the Northern Sung dynasty, was deposed and carried into exile by the Jurchen. This final ignominy has in no way dimmed the emperor's reputation, however, for he is remembered not as an autocrat but as an artist. Among his extant works is a subdued but highly naturalistic study of one of the parakeets in the royal aviary (detail at right). The scroll below, a more ambitious work, reveals Hui Tsung as a great patron of the arts as well. Ladies Preparing Newly-woven Silk is attributed to the emperor, but it is thought to have been copied by him from a work in his own collection. The boldly colored work depicts women beating silk fibers with flails (right), drawing out the threads (center), and ironing a completed bolt of cloth (left).

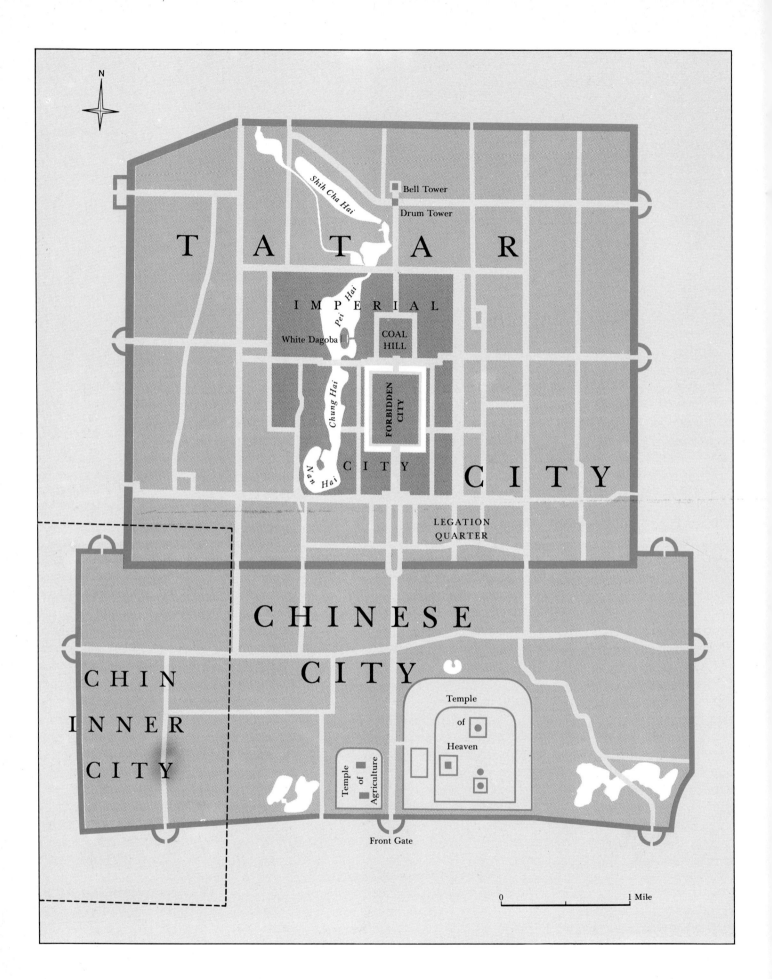

ments. They reserved the key government posts for Jurchen, deliberately limiting the number that could be filled by Chinese and purging the Chin army of non-Jurchen personnel. A full-fledged Chinese examination system was set up, but prospective bureaucrats from among the Jurchen did not have to brave it. Some twenty-five years after the move to Chung-tu, the Chin emperor decreed that all Jurchen who had adopted Chinese surnames or Chinese attire should be punished.

All such punitive measures were to no avail, however, for in the vast northern plain the Jurchen were outnumbered even more hopelessly than the Khitan had been. A substantial Jurchen migration into the plain did little to rectify the balance, and in the long run did much to acclimatize the Jurchen to Chinese society. The decision to move the central capital to Yenching in 1153 had symbolized the Chin dynasty's acceptance of the fact that theirs was essentially a Chinese empire, albeit alien ruled. An even more concrete acknowledgment of the "Chineseness" of the empire was the construction at Chung-tu of a Chinese-style capital, created with the help of the great Sung architects and artisans whom the Chin had captured at Kaifeng.

The Chin took the north wall of the Liao city as a fixed line and expanded the city to the east, south, and west. The new city was almost a square in shape, its four walls covering a distance of some twenty miles as compared with the twelve miles of the Liao city. In each wall were three gates. Using the foundations of the former Liao palace as a starting point, and expanding them as they had expanded the city walls, the Chin built an almost-square, walled inner city, about five and a half miles in circumference and slightly off-cen-

ter in relation to the outer city. This was the Imperial City, where the emperor and his court lived. For the construction of its palaces, doors, windows, and special stone were brought all the way from the plundered former capital of Kaifeng. According to the dynastic history, the transportation of a single large piece of timber might cost 200,000 ounces of silver, for much of the wood came from a park 150 miles from Chung-tu. A single wagon might have to be pulled by five hundred men. The palaces were decorated in gold and in five colors, and a single palace might cost hundreds of millions of ounces of silver. Equally enormous was the number of lives lost among the 800,000 laborers and 400,000 soldiers employed in the construction.

The greater part of the city was occupied by palaces or forbidden areas and very few ordinary citizens lived there. Even sophisticated visitors from the Sung were impressed by a court that in some respects exceeded their own in grandeur. One Sung diplomat reported that "the walls were hung with tapestries of embroidered dragons, and the beams and girders were clothed in embroidery. . . . There were innumerable palace structures in front and behind, extravagant beyond measure and built with infinite artistry."

The first imperial capital on the site of Peking must indeed have been a magnificent sight. Unhappily, little of that city remains today, for in 1215 the armies of Genghis Khan attacked Chung-tu, looted its palaces, and put the Chin capital to fire and the sword.

III

The Great Interior

The fires lit by the Mongols burned on and off for a month, gradually reducing the Chin capital of Chung-tu to smoldering ashes. The charred ruins of the city were bitter evidence of the danger of establishing an imperial Chinese capital so vulnerably close to the steppe. But even before its destruction the Chin had abandoned Chung-tu. After an earlier Mongol attack, the wary Chin emperor had transferred his court to the old Sung capital of Kaifeng. At that point, the future of Chung-tu looked far gloomier than that of Ch'ang-an after its capture by An Lu-shan. Unlike Ch'ang-an, Chung-tu did not have the natural defenses to make it an ideal capital — and both ruling dynasties, the Chin and the Southern Sung, located capitals far to the south of the hostile steppe, protected respectively by the Yellow and Yangtze rivers. Nor did the Mongols show any signs of imitating their nomad predecessors, the Khitan and the Jurchen, by setting up a major capital on the North China plain; they used Chung-tu only as a regional administrative center.

For Genghis Khan, the whole idea of a great metropolitan capital was probably quite strange. The true capital of his vast empire was the saddle of his horse; from that vantage he directed campaigns that swept across the Eurasian land mass. Genghis left it to his successor, Ogadai, to turn the Mongol camp at Karakorum, north of the Gobi Desert, into a capital. Friar William of Rubruck, an emissary of Louis IX of France who arrived in Karakorum in 1254 — eighteen years after its inauguration as the capital of Ogadai's khanate — was less than impressed by the city:

Of the city of Caracarum you must know that exclusive of the palace of the Chan [Khan], it is not as big

as the village of Saint Denis, and the monastery of Saint Denis is ten times larger than the palace. . . . And the palace is like a church, with middle nave, and two sides beyond two rows of pillars, and with three doors to the south, and beyond the middle door on the inside stands the tree, and the Chan sits in a high place to the north, so that he can be seen by all; and two rows of steps go up to him; by one he who carries his cup goes up, and by the other he comes down. The space which is in the middle between the trees and these steps by which they go up to him is empty; for here stands his cup-bearer, and also envoys bearing presents; and he himself sits up there like a divinity.
. . . The palace extends from the north [southward].

Although the Mongols captured Kaifeng, extinguished the Chin dynasty, and established themselves in control of the northern plain before the construction of Karakorum began, they did not build their capital within the borders of China. The reason presumably lay in the extent of the Mongol empire. Genghis Khan's conquests, stretching from the Volga to the Amur, had been divided among three sons and a grandson. Ogadai was the supreme Great Khan, but he ruled directly only the eastern section of the empire — Mongolia and North China. If he were to retain a meaningful overlordship of the whole of Genghis Khan's legacy, his capital could hardly be located in China, almost four thousand miles from the western frontier of the khanate of the Golden Horde in Russia. Conquest by the Mongols seemed to have ended the brief glory of Chung-tu as an imperial capital.

Then, in the mid-1200's, certain centrifugal forces began to assert themselves. As the Mongol empire

stopped expanding, the four khans who had divided Genghis's lands became rulers rather than conquerors, and they were compelled to grapple with the particular problems of their domains. Kublai, grandson of Genghis, was the first Great Khan to devote his attention primarily to China. It was he who pressed the campaign against the Southern Sung to a victorious conclusion, bringing all of China under Mongol rule in 1279. And it was he who changed the Mongol line of Great Khans into an orthodox Chinese dynasty with the dynastic title of Yüan and with such customary Chinese titles as "Grand Progenitor" (posthumously conferred upon Genghis Khan) and "Regenerating Progenitor" (Kublai himself). He ordered the adoption of Chinese court ceremonial, and he moved the Mongol capital to the site of modern Peking less than thirty years after Ogadai had ordered the construction of Karakorum.

Kublai visited Ta-hsing — Chung-tu's new name under the Mongols — just after his election as Great Khan in 1260. He may have toyed with the idea of rebuilding the old Chin city as his capital at that time, for in the following year repairs were made to its walls. But by the time he returned in 1263, he had evidently decided to build afresh. He ordered the construction of a central capital with new walls, a new moat, and a palace — and shortly thereafter workmen began constructing the new capital a little to the northeast of where Chung-tu had stood.

The new site was linked in prophetic legend with the Mongols. About the time of Genghis Khan's birth, Chin geomancers heard of a hill of propitious proportions somewhere north of the imperial frontier. They believed this hill possessed a "king-making vital force" that could be to the Chin's disadvantage. Unable to devise a means of combating its influence, they decided that the only solution was to transfer the hill to Chin territory. Accordingly, they sent presents to the Mongols who controlled the area and asked for permission to remove the hill on the grounds that it would enable the Chin to suppress evil spirits. The Mongols, much amused, agreed, and Chin troops in large numbers dug up the hill, carried the earth to a spot north of the city wall, and there piled it up into a hill again. They then planted flowers and trees upon it and dug a lake around it.

A more sober, modern explanation of the origin of the artificial hill is that there was once a natural lake on the site, and that in the course of deepening it, excavated mud was piled up to form an island. The Liao may have built a palace in the area, and the Chin are known to have ornamented the island with marble pillaged from the Sung imperial gardens in Kaifeng. The mound became known as the Island of Flowered Jade. The island and the lake became part of the grounds of a Chin palace of almost one hundred rooms that was built in 1179 on the east bank of the lake. This seems to have been the first important building on what was to become the site of the Forbidden City. The Chin used this Palace of Ten Thousand Tranquillities — to give it the last of its many names — as their summer resort, but the Mongol Yüan and their successors were to make it the location of their winter residence.

The imperial summer palace did not escape unscathed during the Mongol assault on the Chin capital, and there is evidence to suggest that the defenders

One of the earliest descriptions of Ta-tu, the Mongol capital, was written by Rashid al-Din, an Arab statesman who visited the Great Khan's court in the late thirteenth century. The miniature below, which appeared in a 1314 edition of Rashid's History of the World, portrays a band of thickset Mongol horsemen in battle dress. The loyal troops who rode into battle alongside Genghis Khan also rode with him on his final journey, as the Persian miniature at right reveals. To ensure that the Great Khan's remains would not be defiled, his officers carried his coffin (center) to a remote burial ground, where it was secretly interred.

themselves pulled down three of its halls in 1212 so that the timber could be used for firewood within the besieged city. Like the nearby capital, the palace was attacked and captured in 1215, but it escaped the utter destruction visited upon Chung-tu, possibly because it was outside the walls and the Mongols concentrated all their fury on the city itself. When Kublai Khan visited the area in 1260, the old Palace of Ten Thousand Tranquillities was probably the only surviving construction fit to serve as a Great Khan's court. Some scholars believe that Kublai may have actually lived on the Island of Flowered Jade, in a palace known as the Hall of the Moon, during this period. If so, it may well have been the inherent charm of these surroundings that eventually persuaded him to shift the site of his capital southeast from Karakorum.

The city wall, the new capital's main line of defense, was naturally the first thing built, and 382 families were reportedly displaced before it was completed in 1267. The thirteenth-century Arab statesman and historian Rashid al-Din has left an account of how these walls were made:

> The ramparts of the city . . . are formed of earth. The custom of the country in making such ramparts is first to set up planks, and then to fill in moist earth between them, ramming it hard with great wooden rammers; they then remove the planks, and the earth remains forming a solid wall.

In 1268, temporary palace walls were put up; three years later a work force of over 28,000 laborers replaced them with the palace's final walls. The main halls of the palace were not begun until 1273, but were completed in a year. The speed with which this part of the enterprise was carried out suggests that considerable use must have been made of the old Palace of Ten Thousand Tranquillities, or at least of its foundations.

On the lunar New Year's Day — which fell on February 9 in 1274 — Kublai Khan visited the main hall of the palace and received general congratulations on the successful conclusion of his massive enterprise. The felicitations were somewhat premature, however, for the work was not yet over. In 1281, four thousand soldiers of the imperial bodyguard are said to have completed work — perhaps only repairs — on the main hall; and the finishing touches were not put on the city wall (which was roughly seventeen and a half miles in circumference) until 1292, only two years before Kublai Khan's death.

The new capital was called Ta-tu, "Great Capital." It had been planned and supervised by a Moslem architect whom the Chinese called Yeh-hei-tieh-erh, but like Karakorum it was built along Chinese lines. Work had begun only after a topographical analysis had been made on the basis of geomancy, and the city had then been laid out in districts, with the palace of the emperor along the central north-south axis facing the auspiciously sunny south.

The imperial palace was called the *ta nei,* or "Great Interior"; under succeeding dynasties the term would be changed to Forbidden City. The Great Interior was the innermost of the enclosed cities of Ta-tu. Within the main city wall was the Hsiao rampart, named after a heroic Liao empress, which enclosed the whole complex of palaces, gardens, and lakes that later became known as the Imperial City. The Venetian adventurer Marco Polo, who arrived in Ta-tu with his father and uncle a year after the official completion of the capital, described this rampart as "a very thick wall and fully ten paces in height. It is all white-washed and battlemented." The slightly longer east-west walls probably measured about a mile and a half, and there was an indentation at the southwest corner.

Within the Imperial City was the Palace City; it too was enclosed by a thirty-six-foot-high wall. According to Polo, both walls were defended by what he floridly called "palaces" — which were, apparently, mere watchtowers. There were eight to each wall — one over each corner, and one over four different gates. Each watchtower was used for the storage of different military supplies: in one were saddles, bridles, and other tack; in another, archery equipment; in a third, armor.

The precise dimensions of the Palace City, like those of the Imperial City, are still a subject of scholarly debate, but the enclosure probably measured somewhat under half a mile from east to west and a good thousand yards from north to south. Access was provided by six gates, one each in the north, east, and west walls, and three in the south. The central southern gate had three openings — which led Polo to say that the south wall had five gates. The great central opening was reserved for the emperor; through it he entered the heart of the Great Interior, a collection of buildings that were grouped around two main halls. These in turn were set along a central north-south axis and surrounded by a gallery pierced by gates.

When Marco Polo described Kublai Khan's palace as the "largest that was ever seen." he was almost certainly referring not to the Great Interior but to the more important of the two main halls, the Chamber of

the Great Light. This was the throne room used for coronations and for the major celebrations at the beginning of a new year and on the emperor's birthday. It measured 210 feet from east to west and 126 feet from north to south, and its ceiling was 94½ feet high; it was surrounded by a marble veranda, 46 feet wide and 52½ feet high, the outer edge of which was supported by columns. The whole building was eleven feet above the ground. Marble staircases, one on each side, led to the veranda and to the throne room.

Extensive apartments at the back of the palace served as treasure chambers and as quarters for Kublai's wives and concubines. The Franciscan ascetic, Friar Odoric of Pordenone, who spent three years in Ta-tu in the 1320's, states that there were twenty-four columns of gold in the palace and that its walls were hung with skins of red leather. Chinese sources suggest that it was only screens that were hung with leather and that this took place only during the winter.

More precise descriptions of the Chamber of the Great Light are provided by Chinese documents from the era. A Ming bureaucrat sent to survey the Yüan palaces after the Mongols had been driven from Ta-tu gave this account:

> The bases of the columns are in green peppered stone, and the upper pediments of alabaster and the surrounding railing is of grained stone. The floor is covered with double carpets. The red beams are painted with gold, with carved dragons on them. On all sides are red carved windows bordered with rings. The ceiling is painted in gold and decorated. The double flight of steps are in marble and the red balustrades are gilded. Under a copper flying eagle is placed the seven-jewelled imperial throne in designs of clouds and dragons. The throne has a white cover and a cushion of cloth of gold.

The Chamber of the Great Light dominated the front, or southern, section of the Great Interior, which included other important buildings. To the rear of these buildings — that is, to the north, through two sets of gates — was a group of four more buildings, including the other major hall. This structure was smaller than the Chamber of the Great Light in length and breadth, but it was taller, probably two stories high.

Outside the walls of the Palace City but within the Imperial City stood Marco Polo's Green Hill. A hundred paces high and over a mile in circumference, the Green Hill was constructed of earth dredged from the lake to the west of the Great Interior. Here the khan had planted trees, principally evergreens, from different parts of China. The grounds were paved with lapis lazuli to intensify the green of the trees and at the summit was a handsome green palace. Bretschneider, the renowned nineteenth-century specialist on the history of Peking, argued that Polo's Green Hill was in fact the hill on the Island of Flowered Jade, basing his assertion on the fact that he could find no separate reference to such a hill in Chinese sources written before the sixteenth century. However, contemporary Chinese sources trace today's Coal Hill back to a Yüan dynasty Green Hill. If that is the case, then the Green Hill lay on the city's central north-south axis, where it served to protect Kublai from the unpropitious influences of the cold and gloomy north.

Surrounding the Green Hill was the Divine Menagerie, a park where white harts, musk deer, roebuck, stags, squirrels, and other animals wandered. Kublai could walk through this park on paved paths, which were raised above ground level so that mud and rainwater would not collect on them. To the west of the park and the Great Interior was the lake, about a mile and a quarter from north to south and teeming with a great variety of fish. A wooden bridge led from the shore to an island known today as the Round City, and from the island a marble bridge led north to the Island of Flowered Jade, renamed the Hill of Ten Thousand Years in 1271. The east-west crossing was completed from the Round City by way of another long wooden bridge. On the west bank were two other palaces, one belonging to the heir apparent and one to the empress dowager. According to Marco Polo, the heir apparent's palace was in the same style and on the same scale as Kublai's own.

Outside the wall of the Imperial City was the city proper. The young Venetian was entranced by it:

> . . . the streets are so broad and straight that from the top of the wall above one gate you can see along the whole length of the road to the gate opposite. The city is full of fine mansions, inns, and dwelling-houses. All the way down the sides of every main street are booths and shops of every sort. All the building sites throughout the city are square and measured by the rule; and on every site stand large and spacious mansions with ample courtyards and gardens . . . the whole interior of the city is laid out in squares like a chess-board with such masterly precision that no description can do justice to it.

Despite his enthusiasm, Marco Polo failed to point out

one simple device used by the city's planners to increase the comfort of the citizens of the capital. The great avenues were laid out from east to west; most of the north-south arteries in the grid pattern were short and narrow. The objective was to obtain maximum benefit from southern exposure and to minimize the impact of the cold northern winds that swept the area in winter.

Two great buildings flanked the Imperial City and emphasized its centrality. To the east was the Imperial Ancestral Temple, where Kublai and his successors offered sacrifices to their forebears; to the west was the Altar of Earth and Grain. To the north — placed so that the activity of commerce, which the Chinese considered vulgar, could be carried on behind the emperor, out of his range of vision — was the city's main market. In the market, at the precise center of the city, stood the Bell Tower. (The Drum Tower, once its neighbor, still stands on its original site, but the Bell Tower was moved north to its present site during the Ming dynasty.) Marco Polo tells us that the bell was sounded three times every evening to announce the start of the curfew. Only under very extenuating circumstances, such as childbirth or severe illness, was anyone allowed to break curfew. Cavalry troops, thirty to forty strong, patrolled the city to arrest anyone violating the law; offenders were beaten with a rod.

The positioning of the main temples and the market underlined Kublai Khan's determination to construct his capital according to the traditional canons of Chinese city planning. The classical statement of these canons is found in the *Rites of Chou,* a Confucian reconstruction of customs under the Chou dynasty:

> The capital city is a rectangle of nine square *li*. On each side of the wall there are three gates. . . . The Altar of Ancestors is to the left [east], and that of Earth, right [west]. The court is held in front, and marketing is done in the rear.

True, Ta-tu was not a perfect square and it had only eleven, not twelve gates. Nevertheless, this capital, built by an alien ruler and his alien city planners, conformed more closely to the ritual ideal than did Ch'ang-an, the creation of two native Chinese dynasties, the Sui and the T'ang. The imperial palace at Ch'ang-an had been set against the north wall, which was short one gate. The two main markets were located in front of the palace, an arrangement that made it easier to handle goods coming in through the city's east and west gates. Perhaps the Sui and T'ang, as indigenous dynasties, had the self-confidence to sanction deviations from the native tradition, a self-confidence that the alien Yüan, striving to approximate the Chinese dynastic pattern, did not possess.

Whatever differences there were in the overall plans of Ch'ang-an and Ta-tu, the two capitals resembled each other in one vital respect: they were both badly sited for provisioning. Ta-tu was located at the fulcrum of Kublai's two empires; one farmland, the other steppe. By 1270, the influx of bureaucrats to the still-uncompleted city had expanded its population to 400,-000. Two years later local food resources proved insufficient to maintain the growing population, and famine threatened. Kublai's fondness for the vast banquets described by Marco Polo aggravated the situation.

The improvement of water transportation within the North China plain failed to solve the problem, for long

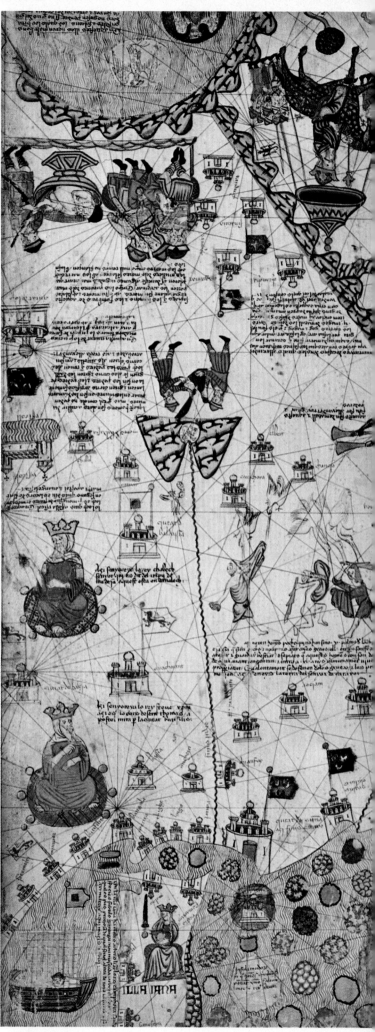

The Catalan Atlas, which was still considered an authoritative guide to the known world decades after its issue in 1375, is composed of eight painted wooden panels, each illustrated in such a manner that it must be viewed from both top and bottom. For example, the lower right quadrant of this panel bears the upside-down label "Catayo." That portion of the map is bisected by the Grand Canal, which runs vertically from "chambalech," or "City of the Great Khan," to the sea.

years of warfare had so decimated the agriculture of the area that it faced famine almost every year. Even the conquest of the Lower Yangtze rice bowl in 1276 did not ameliorate the situation, because the old Sui-T'ang canal system was in considerable disrepair. In 1277 there were crop failures in two northern provinces, and another famine ensued. Like the Sui emperors some seven hundred years earlier, Kublai came to realize that to make his capital viable he would have to ensure the swift transportation of grain from the southern rice bowl.

Unlike the Sui, Kublai had a choice of methods. With Ta-tu relatively close to the coast, grain could be brought north by sea as well as by canal. This should have been a cause for satisfaction at the Yüan court; in fact it resulted in bitter bureaucratic infighting that persisted even after the Great Khan's death.

The government first tried canals. The one built by the Sui (see map, page 60) to supply troops along the frontier was too circuitous, involving a detour of hundreds of miles. A more direct route had to be constructed. Under the Sung, a spur had been added to the Grand Canal to link Huai-yin to Tsining in western Shantung. In 1280, it was decided to lengthen this spur northward by fifty miles to link it to the Ta-ch'ing River. On reaching the river, grain ships would then be able to sail down to the sea and then up the coast to Chih-ku near modern Tientsin. Another plan called for a widening of the Chiao-lai River, whose hundred-mile length neatly severed the neck of the Shantung peninsula, to enable northbound grain ships to avoid the long and dangerous detour around the peninsula. Money was allocated for both projects, local labor

was conscripted, and 100,000 men from the recently defeated Sung armies were sent north to lend their many hands. Then, early in 1282, the scheme came to an abrupt halt when the supervising minister, Achmach Bailo, was murdered.

The assassination of Achmach Bailo was a great cause célèbre of Kublai's reign. The facts of the case, as deduced from the conflicting accounts contained in Chinese and Persian sources as well as in *The Book of Marco Polo,* are these: Achmach Bailo, a top government minister for many years, was killed by a group of Chinese conspirators led by a senior army officer. The plotters, who acted while Kublai was in his summer capital at Shang-tu, appear to have been motivated partly by antiforeign sentiments but principally by fury at Achmach's oppressive rule. (If the canal construction methods of the Sui are anything to go by, Achmach's responsibility for the building of the new canal could have been a major cause of his unpopularity.) His assassins were executed, but when Kublai learned about Achmach Bailo's misrule the latter's corpse was disinterred, beheaded, and left for dogs to eat. Achmach's junior colleagues were disgraced and the Yüan canal-building program sustained a major setback.

At this point, two ex-pirates who had put five hundred ships at the disposal of the Mongols in their final campaigns against the Sung offered their services. They reminded the government that in 1276 they had arranged for the booty of Hangchow to be transported to Ta-tu by sea and suggested they would do the same with grain. The plan was accepted, and the first shipment of some three thousand tons of grain arrived at Chih-ku in April 1283.

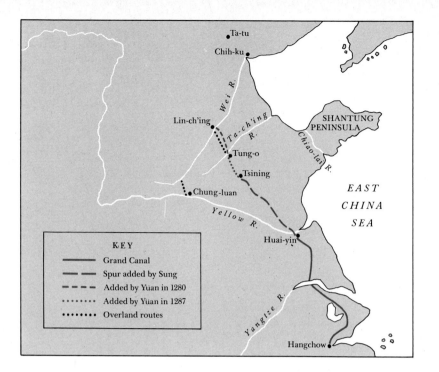

KEY
— Grand Canal
– – Spur added by Sung
- - - Added by Yuan in 1280
· · · · · Added by Yuan in 1287
•••••• Overland routes

The cargo was badly needed in the capital, for there had been another food shortage during the preceding winter. The shipment was only a drop in the bucket, however; in January 1283, the Grand Secretariat had met in emergency session and calculated that every year some 145,000 tons of grain would have to be brought to the capital from the south. The current inland route, which involved pulling the food barges up the Yellow River as far inland as Chung-luan, then transporting them overland sixty miles before they could be put back on ships and sent down the Wei River to Chih-ku, was only able to furnish the capital with 22,000 tons. It was decided to deepen the canal between the Yellow and Wei rivers in order to cut out the time-consuming overland section, and it was also decided to recommence work on the plans for two canals across Shantung. The Directorate of Grain Transportation was reorganized for the task and its old officials were sacked.

Kublai gave his personal backing to the new scheme, and his workmen were harried into working quickly by the most brutal methods. Extending the spur of the old Sung canal from Tsining to the Ta-ch'ing River proved difficult because of the high intervening ground. The new waterways were completed in three months — by September 1283 — but it soon became apparent that keeping the entrances of the Ta-ch'ing and Chiao-lai rivers open was going to be a major problem, for sandbars quickly accumulated in those areas. In November the Grand Secretariat had to approve a plan for bypassing the Ta-ch'ing River, newly dredged at a substantial human toll, and sending the grain overland from Tung-o to Lin-ch'ing on the Wei River. The propo-

nents of the canal routes received a further setback when one of their strongest supporters at court was murdered on the high seas, possibly at the instigation of the two ex-pirates, who had many contacts among the sailors of the Mongol fleet. By May 1285, the Chiao-lai River route across the Shantung peninsula had been abandoned and two years later the Ta-ch'ing route was also given up, presumably because of recurring difficulties with the sandbars. The Directorate of Grain Transportation was again reorganized, and the leading proponents of canals were transferred to military units in Annam — where the principal backer of the canal-building scheme was killed in battle.

Chu Ch'ing and Chang Hsuan, the ex-pirates, were by then two of the wealthiest men in South China. They charged such exorbitant rates for transporting the vital grain that shipping costs were often three times the price of the grain itself. Unfortunately for them, twenty-five per cent of the sea-borne shipment was lost in a typhoon in the summer of 1286 — a disaster that coincided with one of the worst famines in North China in years. Early in 1287, at a time when the dismissal of the canal bureaucrats should have enabled Chu Ch'ing and Chang Hsuan to amass even greater wealth, they were pushed aside by the new prime minister, an Uighur named Sangga. Sangga, who realized that it was foolish to depend upon just one method of shipment, decided to open a canal between Tung-o and Lin-ch'ing so as to complete an inland water route from the Yangtze to Ta-tu; at the same time he set a goal of 73,000 tons of grain to be brought each year by sea. The target was almost achieved in 1289 and in 1290, and in the two subsequent years the amount of grain

brought by the sea route was around 110,000 tons.

The construction of the new canal was not attended with similar success. The problems were immense and continuous effort was required to keep the canal open. Tens of thousands of tons of grain could be transported by this route, but the sea route remained the principal source of supply. Ironically enough under the circumstances, it was a failure on the sea route — the loss of sixteen per cent of the shipment of 1291 — that brought down Sangga and his clique. In the wake of that disaster, the Directorate of Grain Transportation was reorganized yet again — and Chu Ch'ing and Chang Hsuan were reinstated. By sending their ships by a deep-sea route instead of along the dangerous and circuitous coastal route, they managed to cut the sea journey from one or two months to ten days. The first coastal grain ships had held either twenty or seventy-five tons; now supertransports capable of carrying almost six hundred tons could be used. By 1310, the annual sea shipments had reached about 220,000 tons, and in 1329 the figure hit a record of 255,000 tons.

By that time Chu Ch'ing and Chang Hsuan, whose arrogance and power had angered bureaucrats in the capital, were no longer in charge. After the death of Kublai in 1294, they were no longer needed to provide ships for the Great Khan's grandiose naval expeditions, and their enemies acted. In 1302, they were accused of treason; Chu responded by committing suicide, Chang was executed. Two new men, Moslem aliens, brought about the transportation feats of the next thirty years.

Ta-tu, like Ch'ang-an before it, had become parasitically dependent on the Yangtze rice bowl. But from 1330 onward, insurrections in that southern area gravely affected grain supplies. Matters got worse when the sea route was disrupted by a pirate named Fang Kuo-chen in 1348, and they grew still worse after 1350, when warfare became almost continuous in the south. By 1359, grain shipments were reduced to almost nothing and attempts to develop the Hai River near modern Tientsin into a second Yangtze basin proved unavailing. Floods and famine in the Yellow River region exacerbated the crisis and it seems likely that sharply rising grain prices contributed heavily to the currency devaluation that increasingly disrupted the economy and demoralized the Yüan administration.

The disruption of grain supplies underlined the problems of maintaining a capital in the Peking area. Yet the Chin dynasty had been able to maintain itself in North China in the face of repeated attempts by the Southern Sung, who controlled the Yangtze rice bowl, to dislodge them. Over the centuries, the Peking area had been shown to be highly vulnerable to attack from the steppe, but the Yüan was the first major dynasty with its capital there to be overthrown by an attack from the south. Why did the Yüan fail where the Chin had succeeded, and fail less than seventy-five years after the death of the great Kublai?

The reasons are to be found in the Mongols' refusal to come fully to terms with their Chinese environment. At first it looked as if things might turn out differently, for the Mongol conquest owed much to the employment of Chinese and Khitan defectors from the Chin empire, and such men were used as administrators as more Chin territory was acquired. A Sinicized scion of the Khitan royal clan, Yeh-lü Ch'u-ts'ai, became one of Genghis Khan's chief advisers, and after

His contemporaries called Kublai Khan "Regenerating Progenitor," but the honorific proved a misnomer: the Yüan dynasty did not long survive its most vigorous and visionary leader. During Kublai's lifetime, however, the swarthy, broad-faced ruler (left) infused his administration with a special dynamism, pursuing statecraft and game with the same unbridled enthusiasm. The detail at right, from a Yüan dynasty scroll, records a royal hunt. Kublai appears at center, clad in ermine.

1229 he was entrusted by Genghis's son, Ogadai, with organizing the administration of the captured Chin territories. Yeh-lü Ch'u-ts'ai's first great achievement was to frustrate the serious suggestion, made by a section of the Mongol court, that they kill all the Chinese and turn North China's farmlands into pasturelands for Mongol herds and flocks. This he prevented, not by appealing to the Mongols' better natures, but by arousing their cupidity, arguing that the taxation of North China's fifty million people would yield much more wealth than would stock breeding.

Repeating advice given to the first Han emperor — "The empire has been conquered on horseback, but it cannot be governed on horseback" — Yeh-lü Ch'u-ts'ai attempted to convince his Mongol masters to reinstitute a complete Chinese-style administration. Despite some limited successes, Yeh-lü Ch'u-ts'ai never succeeded in his objective. The Mongols persisted in regarding the territories they were assigned to administer as their personal fiefs, keeping the taxes for themselves. The former personal chancellery of the Great Khan was renamed and recognized as the supreme Chinese-style administrative office, and Chinese titles were conferred upon native officials. But Yeh-lü Ch'u-ts'ai's attempt to restore the examination system in order to recruit bureaucrats by merit — the essential basis of the Chinese administrative system — was soon abandoned.

It was not until the reign of Kublai that a truly powerful and centralized administration was established. The secretariat became once more the supreme governmental body, and taxes were collected for the central government. Yet even Kublai did not restore the examination system, preferring to rely upon a cadre of foreign civil servants, such as Achmach Bailo, Sangga, and Marco Polo himself.

Reflected through the prism of Marco Polo's enthusiastic vision, Kublai Khan looms twice as large as life. Not that Polo tried to exaggerate Kublai's personal appearance; indeed, his portrait is remarkably faithful:

He is a man of good stature, neither short nor tall but of moderate height. His limbs are well fleshed out and modelled in due proportion. His complexion is fair and ruddy like a rose, the eyes black and handsome, the nose shapely and set square in place.

But Polo's description of Kublai's palace, his court and his banquets, his splendid capital and his great empire, lifts the Great Khan off the pages of history and gives him a three-dimensional quality that most other Chinese emperors lack. It was this quality, doubtless, that inspired Coleridge to raise the human "Kubla Khan" to an almost mystical level.

None of this can disguise the fact that it was Kublai, for all his gifts, who ensured the collapse of the Mongol empire. Precisely because he was superior to most of his line, precisely because he saw the need to adapt to the Chinese environment, he should have anticipated that it was essential to integrate the natural leaders of the indigenous population into the Yüan dynasty. Instead, he restricted Chinese to lower administrative posts and allowed the perpetuation of a caste system in which Mongols and their foreign aides ranked above northern Chinese, while the southern Chinese, proud heirs to the glorious Sung cultural tradition, ranked lowest of all.

Marco Polo, as a Yüan official, was in a position to sense the effect of Mongol apartheid, and he reported

that "all the Cathayans hated the government of the Great Khan, because he set over them Tartar rulers, mostly Saracens, and they could not endure it, since it made them feel that they were no more than slaves." Liu Yin, one of the most brilliant men of his time and one of the few "Cathayans," or northern Chinese, to whom Kublai was prepared to give high office, indicated in a poem why he spurned the Great Khan's suggestion:

When one is born in a degenerate and disorderly
    age
And there is no one worthy of being called a
    ruler, who would want to serve?

The southern Chinese, inhabitants of an area the Mongols called Manzi, were even more embittered. Cheng Ssu-hsiao, who would probably have had a distinguished official career under the Southern Sung but for the Mongol conquest, devoted his life to the denigration of the victors and the praise of the vanquished. One of his poems declares:

In the past, in the age of the former emperor,
Who faced the sun for forty years,
The bright light of learning and refinement
    flooded the world,
And superior and heroic men stood before their
    ruler.
But once the barbarian soldiers invaded,
With sudden shock, Han rule was toppled.
To this day the proper ways of men are in chaos.
To lonely mountain valleys have fled all the
    worthies of the former age.

Hatred of a usurping dynasty and loyalty to an overthrown one may not sound odd to Westerners, but those sentiments ran counter to a fundamental Chinese political concept — the mandate of heaven. According to this ancient doctrine, dynasties waxed and waned because of the personalities and deeds of their rulers, and dynasties were overthrown because the faults and errors of their last emperors had lost them the mandate of heaven. It was not a completely satisfactory explanation of the observable Chinese dynastic cycle, for it neglected economic factors, but as developed by Confucian theorists such as Mencius the doctrine allowed bureaucrats to abandon a decadent emperor and accept office under a new dynasty. Yeh-lü Ch'u-ts'ai had felt himself justified in transferring his allegiance from the Chin to the Yüan precisely because the victories of the Mongols were proof to him that the mandate of heaven had been withdrawn from the Chin.

Perhaps if Yeh-lü Ch'u-ts'ai had succeeded in setting up a truly Chinese administration, things might have been different. But there was more than frustration at the lack of employment behind the attitude of the anti-Mongol Chinese. Compared to the two previous alien conquerors of China, the Khitan and the Jurchen, the Mongols were the most nomadic. Kublai even sowed the grass of the steppe in the courtyard of his palace in Ta-tu to remind himself of his origins. The Mongols were thus the most different from their subjects in customs and attitudes. The Chinese found them more offensive than the Khitan or the Jurchen, and yet they had to submit to even greater humiliation and suppression at the Mongols' hands. Accustomed since the late T'ang era to a basically anticlerical government, the Chinese also resented Yüan patronage of the Lamaist Buddhists, who used their special privi-

Kublai Khan's dissolute successors, who abandoned themselves to easy living and the pleasures of the palace (left), exposed the fundamental weakness of the Yüan era: shorn of effective leadership, the dynasty could no longer suppress the rebellion rife in the empire. By 1356, sixty-two years after Kublai's death, the country had been plunged into civil war — and in 1368 Ta-tu fell to a rebel army.
  Overleaf:
The lush, limpid, and intensely cultivated Yangtze valley was Hung Wu's homeland and power base. From this verdant cockpit he launched the drive that ultimately toppled the Yüan and enabled him to establish the Ming dynasty.

leges in an increasingly corrupt manner in the 1300's.

Fueled by this widespread hatred for the alien rulers, uprisings began to take place in the old Southern Sung territories in the 1330's. The Yüan had been weakened through a series of short reigns by dissolute emperors — and by increasing factionalism within the royal family and the Mongol aristocracy. The abandonment of the principle that responsibility was assigned on the basis of merit meant that the dynasty and the ruling elite were unable to renew themselves; nor was there a Confucian meritocracy to buttress the weakening throne. The Mongols had even lost their old martial skills, for after Kublai's failure to conquer Japan and parts of Southeast Asia, his successors had settled down to enjoy court life, abandoning foreign adventures.

In the 1350's, half a dozen major rebel leaders emerged. One of them was Chu Yüan-chang, a poor orphan from the area northwest of Nanking. Mongol legend has it that all Chinese were compelled to have their thumbs cut off at birth to make them incapable of drawing a bow. The last Yüan emperor was supposedly bribed into suspending this law for three months, and during that period Chu Yüan-chang was born. Chu, whose military abilities were clearly on a par with those of Liu Pang, the other commoner who founded a major dynasty, enrolled in a rebel group in 1352. He was soon leading his own army, and over the next sixteen years he was engaged in virtually continuous warfare against both the Yüan and other Chinese contenders for the succession. In September 1368, he occupied Ta-tu and soon afterwards, Shang-tu. But though the capture of the Mongol capitals marked the beginning of his new

Ming dynasty, Chu had no wish to take over the splendid Yüan cities. Hailing from the Yangtze valley, he fully appreciated the crucial importance of that area's grain supplies to the support of a Chinese dynasty. He placed his capital at Ying-t'ien-fu, which his son would rename Nanking, or "Southern Capital."

The lesson of the Southern Sung had apparently been learned. A Chinese dynasty based in the dominant Yangtze economic region, with immediately accessible grain supplies, was in a strong position to hold off invaders from the ever-dangerous steppe. There would be no need to invest men and money in the construction and preservation of lengthy supply routes. Chinese civilization had found what seemed to be its natural center. Ta-tu was renamed Peiping, or "Northern Peace," and resumed its role as a border bastion. There seemed no reason why a native Chinese dynasty should ever place a capital there.

IV

"Where Earth and Sky Meet"

The first Ming emperor — known to posterity by his reign title of Hung Wu, "Vast Military Power" — left an enduring mark upon Peiping. Like the Chin geomancers before him, Hung Wu feared the malign influence of a hostile king-making vital force. He believed that this force resided in the former Yüan capital — an unsurprising suspicion, since the Mongols continued to menace China for decades after their flight from the city — and so, in 1368, after his officials had carefully catalogued the beauties and grandeur of the Yüan Great Interior, Hung Wu ordered it leveled.

Peiping was soon to recover from the effects of Hung Wu's superstitiousness, but the Ming dynasty would bear his stamp throughout the 276 years of its existence. In the West, the name Ming conjures up a vision of delicate porcelain — and a mistier image of the refined society that is thought to have produced it. For many Chinese of the period, however, the years of Ming rule were a time of terror.

The Ming era witnessed the culmination of a process of increasing despotism that had begun under the Sung dynasts. Reacting against the decentralization of power that had weakened their T'ang predecessors and permitted the An Lu-shan revolt, the Sung emperors had arrogated more power to themselves. The virtual liquidation of the old aristocracy during the T'ang period had removed an important check upon imperial autocracy, and the new meritocracy of civil servants was not treated with the same respect. Under the T'ang, an aristocratic premier had been permitted to sit and drink tea when discussing official business with the emperor. Under the Sung, the worthy bureaucrat who filled that role had to stand; a cup of tea was a rare privilege.

A high civilization had modified the full impact of the despotism that existed under the Sung. No such restraint manifested itself under the Mongols, whose brutalization of Chinese society paved the way for the terror of the Ming.

At first the Ming seemed to represent the long-desired return to the traditional, pre-Mongol method of governing through a Confucian meritocracy. One of Hung Wu's early acts was to restore the examination system for the recruitment of civil servants, for example. But in 1380 the emperor made a significant institutional change when he abolished the office of premier after discovering the treachery of the incumbent, Hu Wei-yung. This step increased Hung Wu's personal power by making the heads of all six ministries — Personnel, Revenue, Rites, War, Justice, and Public Works — directly responsible to the throne. To help him cope with the tremendous burden of work he had taken on — in one ten-day period late in his reign, 1,660 documents dealing with 3,391 separate matters were presented to him for imperial approval — Hung Wu recruited the cream of the civil service to act as his grand secretaries. Unlike other civil servants, however, the grand secretaries did not normally attempt to restrain imperial excesses; instead they became identified with the inner court of the emperor.

The supremacy of the sovereign was accentuated by court protocol. The imperial throne was placed on an elevated dais; a reporting official performed the three kneelings and nine prostrations of the obligatory kowtow some distance away. Violations of protocol could result in immediate beatings at the hands of the court eunuchs. In later reigns, such violations of

court etiquette were sometimes punished by death.

Terrorism became a fact of life during the reign of Hung Wu. In disposing of the case of Hu Wei-yung, the emperor had 30,000 people executed, among them anyone even remotely connected with the former premier, whether by family ties or official dealings. Many were tortured first, a process that was refined in Hung Wu's day to permit the victim to survive for some time. A new device of the period involved slowly slicing a person to death with a prescribed 3,357 strokes of the knife; after each ten slices, there was a pause to permit the victim to recover — so that he would be fully aware of the next ten strokes.

An American historian of the Ming, F. W. Mote, has called Hung Wu the "harshest and most unreasonable tyrant in all of Chinese history," a stern denunciation indeed when one remembers that the competition includes Ch'in Shih Huang Ti and Sui Yang Ti. A man of violent temper and proven cruelty, Hung Wu so terrorized his officials that they often fainted when he began to shout at them. Halfway through his reign, government officials got into the habit of saying their last good-byes to their families if they were required at a morning audience, and of exchanging congratulations with fellow officials if they survived till evening.

The effect of Hung Wu's terrorism was to expose the fundamental contradiction of the Chinese polity — its derivation from the conflicting tenets of Legalism and Confucianism. From the hundred schools of philosophy that had flourished during the Warring States period, the rulers of the state of Ch'in had chosen Legalism as their official ideology. The central tenet of Legalism was that sound government could only be guaranteed by an all-powerful ruler who laid down strict laws and backed them up with harsh punishments. A fundamental assumption of Legalism was that man was basically evil.

When the Ch'in finally crushed the other warring states and created the first centralized empire in 221 B.C., they continued to use Legalist doctrines. Shih Huang Ti, the first Chinese emperor, imposed a beneficial unity upon Chinese culture — weights, measures, money coinage, and the writing system were all standardized — but he did it with the brutality sanctioned by the pitiless tenets of Legalism. Similarly, Shih Huang Ti's Great Wall was a justifiable defensive measure, but it was the cause of so much loss of life among the workmen that it later became known as "the longest cemetery in the world."

The Ch'in imperial system survived the overthrow of the hated and short-lived Ch'in dynasty only because it was given a new ethical basis by the successor Han dynasty, which substituted Confucianism for Legalism as the state ideology. Confucius, like the Legalists, had been supremely interested in politics, but he had taught that the object of sound government was the welfare of the people and that its linchpin was the virtuous ruler. Ideally, the virtue of the ruler inspired emulation by his ministers and subjects, thus ensuring a stable and contented state. In place of the Legalist stress on law, Confucius advocated adherence to traditional rites and customs. The political institutions that he favored were those of the feudal Chou empire; he would probably have been horrified by the centralized state created by the Ch'in. Nevertheless, Confucius's disciples of the Han period were delighted to be recruited

The man who seized the mandate of heaven and founded the Ming dynasty in 1368 was more feared than revered. Hung Wu's malignant temperament, accurately portrayed at right, guaranteed that his long reign would be punctuated by outbursts of exceptional cruelty. Ming terrorism had many precedents, however, beginning with the first ruler of a united China, Shih Huang Ti. Renowned as the builder of the Great Wall, the Ch'in emperor also initiated a savage book-burning campaign. In the painting at left, Shih Huang Ti placidly observes the enforcement of his policy.

as bureaucrats after their proscription under the Ch'in, and they acquiesced to the new centralism in return for the dynasty's acknowledgment that the basis of its polity would be Confucian morality and not Legalist force.

This synthesis of the Legalist state and Confucian ideals — which has been aptly characterized as imbuing autocracy with a conscience — was the supreme example of the political genius of the Chinese. It endured, albeit with interruptions, for over two thousand years — proof not only of the brilliance of the synthesis but also of the pragmatism and flexibility by which generations of emperors and bureaucrats made the system work. Even so, the fundamental contradiction between autocracy, the emperor, and its conscience, the Confucian bureaucracy, persisted. For the system to work well, the emperor had to be vigorous and hard-working but prepared to be guided by his officials. In the last analysis, however, the emperor was supreme and could ignore the unwritten contract between himself and the bureaucrats. It was the misfortune of the Chinese of the Ming period that the increased centralization of power and the elevation of the position of the emperor coincided with the seizure of the throne by a man as cruel as Hung Wu.

The dynasty might still have developed differently if Hung Wu's sixteen-year-old grandson and successor, Hui Ti, had managed to retain the throne. He seems to have been benevolently inclined, and his Confucian mentors had persuaded him of the need to decentralize power. Tragically, he was not allowed to experiment for long. His uncle, the prince of Yen, who like An Lu-shan ruled North China from Peiping, rose in revolt. After a civil war that devastated North China,

Hui Ti was forced to disguise himself as a monk and flee Ying-t'ien-fu. His uncle then ascended the throne, giving himself the reign title Yung Lo, "Everlasting Happiness." Supposedly, the magician who had persuaded Yung Lo to rebel cast a great bronze bell, over twenty feet high and some forty-five tons in weight, in celebration of the victory. It may still be seen today in the Great Bell Temple in Peking.

The overthrow of Hui Ti was a key moment in the Ming dynasty. Yung Lo, like his father, Hung Wu, was capable, ambitious, and above all, cruel. He ensured that the despotism of the founder would be perpetuated as the despotism of the dynasty. His usurpation was also the turning point in the history of Peking. The former prince of Yen decided to shift the capital from the potentially disloyal Yangtze basin to his power base in North China. In 1403, Peiping was renamed Shun-t'ien-fu, but it became generally known as Peking, "Northern Capital"; Ying-t'ien-fu became known as Nanking, "Southern Capital."

In 1404, Yung Lo began reconstructing Peking for its new role. The city's appearance had already been considerably modified during his father's reign. Not only had the Great Interior been leveled, but the city had also been reduced in size. The north wall had been rebuilt about two miles farther south and the northernmost gates in the east and west walls had consequently been demolished.

Yung Lo's reconstruction further altered the Yüan capital in two important respects. The southward movement of the city, begun under Hung Wu, was continued, a new southern city wall being built about half a mile farther south. This lengthened the total circum-

A year after his 1403 accession, the corpulent and canny Ming emperor Yung Lo (right) ordered the reconstruction of Peking and the building of the Forbidden City complex (diagram, far right).

ference of the city walls to fourteen and a half miles, but it still left Peking smaller than Ta-tu had been.

Like Ta-tu, Peking consisted of three concentric walled enclosures: the city proper, the Imperial City, and the palaces of the Forbidden City, the equivalent of the Yüan Great Interior. The southern wall of the Yüan city became the southern wall of the Ming Imperial City, while the southern wall of the Great Interior remained as the basis of the southern wall of the Forbidden City (see diagram, page 46). As a result, there was considerable space at Yung Lo's disposal to the south of the Forbidden City. Into this space he moved the Temple of Heaven and the Temple of Agriculture. This meant modifying the classical canons governing city planning, but it tightened the relationship between these two buildings and the Forbidden City and it increased the majesty of the main north-south axis. This axis was no longer central, Yung Lo's second major change being to move it slightly to the east, but it did thread the major gates of the three cities and the principal palaces within the Forbidden City, just as it had during the Yüan period.

The legend goes that when Yung Lo first arrived in his future capital, a famous astrologer presented him with a sealed envelope. That envelope contained a plan for rebuilding the city on strict geomantic principles, with every major structure representing a part of the body of No Cha, a fabulous figure in popular mythology. Yung Lo is said to have followed the instructions carefully, and it is indeed possible to analyze the main axis of Peking in terms of the human body. But the magnificent reality of the axis as it cut its way across the walled cities of Peking overshadowed all myths

about its origins. In Yung Lo's time the axis began at the great central gate in the thirty-five-foot-high southern city wall. This gateway, which took nine years to build, became known as the Ch'ien Men, "Front Gate," but it was officially named the Cheng Yang Men, "Straight-towards-the-Sun Gate." From the Ch'ien Men, the route passed north through the Great Ming Gate to the square in front of the T'ien An Men, "Gate of Heavenly Peace," gateway to the Imperial City. Beyond that barrier stood the Tuan Men, "Gate of Correct Deportment," flanked by the Temple of Heaven and the Temple of Agriculture.

Finally, half a mile from the Ch'ien Men, the axis reached the Wu Men, "Meridian Gate," the entrance to the Tzu Chin Ch'eng, "Purple Forbidden City" (see diagram opposite). Here was the heart of the capital, the empire, and indeed the world — the place where, as one of the classic Chinese texts states, "earth and sky meet, where the four seasons merge, where wind and rain are gathered in, and where yin and yang are in harmony." Here at the axis of the universe the emperor's role was "to stand in the center of the earth and stabilize the people within the four seas," according to the Confucian sage Mencius. The symbolic centrality of the capital and its alignment along the cardinal points of the compass — which made it the "pivot of the four quarters" — was essential to that role. The misleading epithet "purple" (tzu) did not refer to the red walls of the Forbidden City, but to tzu wei, "polestar" — the implication being that the emperor was the central body around which everything on earth revolved. Confucius himself supposedly said: "He who exercises government by means of his virtue may be

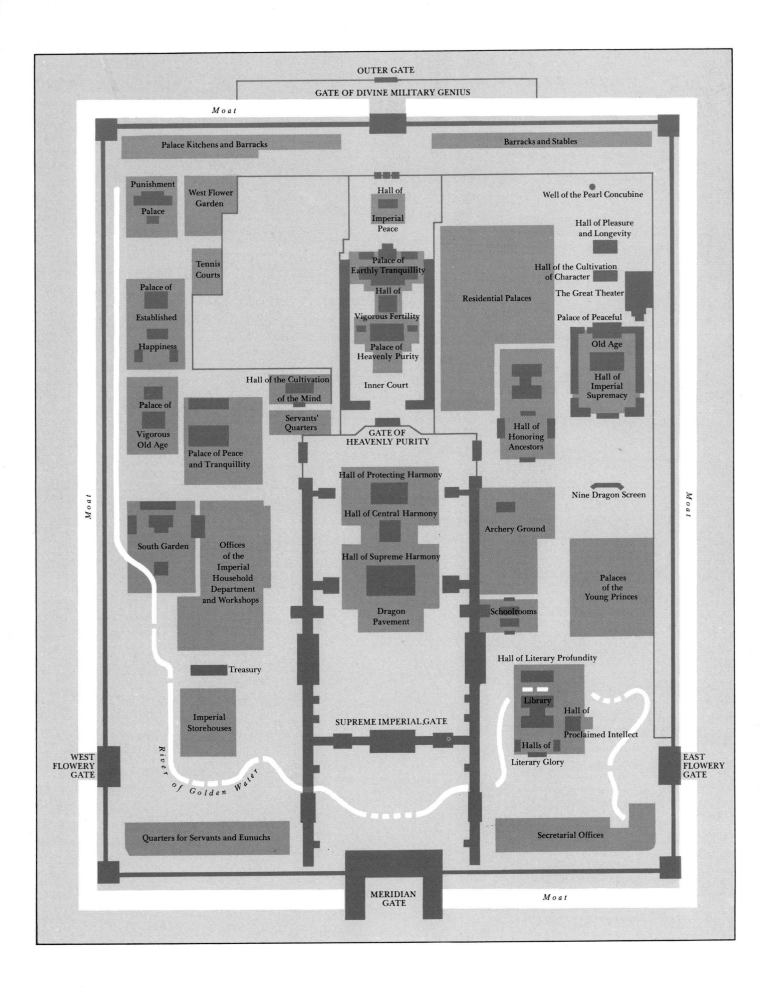

OUTER GATE

GATE OF DIVINE MILITARY GENIUS

Moat

Palace Kitchens and Barracks

Barracks and Stables

Punishment
Palace

West Flower
Garden

Hall of
Imperial
Peace

Well of the Pearl Concubine

Hall of Pleasure
and Longevity

Tennis
Courts

Palace of
Earthly Tranquillity

Hall of the Cultivation
of Character

Palace of

Established

Happiness

Hall of
Vigorous Fertility

Residential Palaces

The Great Theater

Palace of Peaceful

Palace of
Heavenly Purity

Old Age

Palace of

Vigorous
Old Age

Hall of the Cultivation
of the Mind

Inner Court

Hall of
Imperial
Supremacy

Palace of Peace
and Tranquillity

Servants'
Quarters

GATE OF
HEAVENLY PURITY

Hall of
Honoring
Ancestors

Hall of Protecting Harmony

Nine Dragon Screen

South Garden

Offices
of the
Imperial
Household
Department
and Workshops

Hall of Central Harmony

Archery Ground

Hall of Supreme Harmony

Palaces
of the
Young Princes

Schoolrooms

Dragon
Pavement

Treasury

Hall of Literary Profundity

Imperial
Storehouses

Library

Hall of
Proclaimed Intellect

SUPREME IMPERIAL GATE

Halls of

Moat

River of Golden Water

Literary Glory

WEST
FLOWERY
GATE

EAST
FLOWERY
GATE

Quarters for Servants and Eunuchs

Secretarial Offices

MERIDIAN
GATE

Moat

Chinese tolerance of diverse and often incompatible religious doctrines had a profound impact on the arts. The T'ang painting above — in which the Tejaprahba Buddha, seated in a celestial carriage, subdues the five planets — draws heavily upon Buddhist mythology for inspiration. Architecture also benefited from this multiplicity. The unswerving south-north processional way of the Forbidden City (right) was determined by popular rules of geomancy. The same axial principle can be seen in a Ming funerary model (above, right) in which courtyards and pavilions follow the same rigid pattern.

compared to the north pole star, which keeps its place and all the stars turn towards it."

The Forbidden City was approximately one thousand yards from north to south and about eight hundred yards from east to west. Unlike the Yüan Great Interior, it was surrounded by a moat and pierced by four, not six, gates. But like the Great Interior it was divided into two major sections: the first contained the major state buildings; behind this was the residential section. The gates in the east and west walls were placed with uncharacteristic asymmetry in the southern section to provide access to official buildings without disturbing the emperor's privacy.

From the south gate, the Wu Men, the north-south axis continued across a courtyard through which the River of Golden Water flowed. That artificial stream was shaped like a Tatar bow and spanned by five marble bridges. The Pekingese think of the bridges as arrows but actually they were intended to symbolize the five virtues. At the other side of the courtyard was the Huang Chi Men, "Supreme Imperial Gate," the last barrier before the three great ceremonial halls that were the climax of the processional way. These halls of state were set one behind the other on a three-tiered, balustraded, white marble terrace called the Dragon Pavement. Leading up to the terrace, in the middle of the central staircase, was a ramp over which the palanquin of the emperor was carried.

The first and most important of the halls was the setting for special state occasions — the festivities at the beginning of a new year and on the emperor's birthday. The emperor prepared himself for these ceremonies in the second, much smaller hall. In the third hall, the emperor received tributary rulers and scholars who had been successful in the highest civil service examinations.

In the north wall of the great courtyard that surrounded the Dragon Pavement was a gate where Yung Lo gave open-air audiences. Beyond, in the Inner Court, were three great halls corresponding to the three halls on the Dragon Pavement. The first and most important was the residence of the last four Ming emperors, while the third was the residence of their empresses. In between stood the Hall of Vigorous Fertility, which, despite its name and position, was used not for imperial marriage rites but for storing the seals of previous emperors.

The importance of the three main halls of the Inner Court ensured that the northward thrust of the central axis continued on past the Dragon Pavement. Beyond the Forbidden City — but still within the Imperial City — was a great, five-ridged barrier against evil northern influences known as the Hill of Ten Thousand Years. Although it was later renamed Ching Shan, "Prospect Hill," by the Manchus, the mound is generally known by its popular name, Mei Shan, "Coal Hill." In Yung Lo's early years, the spot had indeed been used for storing coal while the Forbidden City was being built.

To the north of Coal Hill, the Gate of Earthly Peace led from the Imperial City to the city proper. Here two more important buildings lay along the main axis. Immediately north of the gate stood the Drum Tower, which was probably a Yüan building, although much restored. Farther north stood Yung Lo's Bell Tower, which had been moved from its former central position to a point just within the city walls. Beyond the tower

loomed the north wall, acting as a final protection against the evil north.

The reconstruction of Peking and the building of the Forbidden City lasted sixteen years, from 1404 to 1420. During this period Peking ranked only as the auxiliary capital. When construction was officially completed on New Year's Day, 1421, the government was moved there and Nanking, containing a duplicate but skeleton administration, became the auxiliary capital. After the death of Yung Lo, the term auxiliary was reapplied to Peking, not because the central government had moved back to Nanking but in anticipation that it would. The Chinese clearly continued to be aware of the drawbacks of situating their capital at Peking, close to the warlike barbarians of the north. From 1437 on, steps were taken to strengthen the defenses of the city. Walls, gates, watchtowers, moats, and bridges were repaired over the course of the next twelve years, the principal task being to add a layer of brick to the walls that had already doubled in thickness under Yung Lo.

The final addition to Ming Peking took place between 1550 and 1565, over a century after the death of Yung Lo, when the southern suburbs were walled in. Strictly speaking, suburbanites were not inhabitants of the city. The Chinese use the same ideogram for city and for wall — an indication of the importance placed upon city walls — and the only true Pekingese were those who lived within the city walls. When the suburbanites' lack of protection was pointed out to the emperor, it was proposed to him that the whole city be surrounded with a new outer wall that would enclose the suburbs. This plan was eventually dropped because of the immense expense it would have involved, but before the plans were changed the southern section of the new wall had been completed and it was decided to join it with the southern wall of the original city. The new outer city bulged rather untidily to both the east and the west, and because it seemed to fit over the inner city like a cap it was also known as "Cap City."

The walling-in operation lengthened Yung Lo's axial line without placing any new buildings across the central avenue. Fortunately, the importance of the southern end of the axis was ensured by the existence of two major structures that flanked the avenue. On the east was Yung Lo's magnificent Temple of Heaven complex, where the Ming rulers sacrificed to the deity by whose mandate their dynasty held the throne. The Chou emperors had been the first to call themselves the Sons of Heaven, and the ideogram for heaven — which includes the ideogram for man — probably originally denoted the ancestors of the Chou imperial line. Long before the time of Yung Lo, however, that term had come to represent a more universal and supernatural, albeit still anthropomorphic, supreme deity. Opposite the Temple of Heaven stood the sixteenth-century Temple of Agriculture, where the emperor came every spring to plough the ritual eight furrows and sow them with sacred rice to guarantee the year's harvest.

Over the centuries, there has been much reconstruction along Peking's central axis. Many of the buildings of the Forbidden City, in their present form, date from Manchu times, but the axis itself is basically the great processional way constructed under Yung Lo. One can still appreciate why no man advancing along it, be he Chinese subject or foreign vassal, could have been in

77

any doubt as to the might and majesty of the reigning emperor. It was an appropriate setting for a dynasty that called itself Ming, or "Illustrious," and in many ways Yung Lo gave the dynasty an impressive second start in its new capital.

In foreign policy, Yung Lo also made a substantial contribution. He sent great imperial fleets across the Indian Ocean and the Arabian Sea for the first time in Chinese history. Chinese naval power, which dated from the Sung era, grew after that dynasty was expelled from North China and began to take greater interest in Southeast Asia. Trade expanded, and the ports of Canton and Ch'uanchou with it. Kublai Khan, although more interested in conquest than commerce, maintained China's naval strength. Then from 1405 on, Yung Lo sent out six naval expeditions under the Moslem eunuch Cheng Ho. The earliest reached Calicut on the west coast of India, and later ones journeyed over five thousand miles — as far as the Persian Gulf, Aden, and the east coast of Africa. On the first expedition alone, Cheng Ho's fleet consisted of sixty-two ships, some up to 2,500 tons in weight, with a total of 28,000 men on board as well as much gold and treasure to distribute to prospective tributaries of the Son of Heaven. Ninety years later, Vasco da Gama arrived in Calicut with three ships, none more than three hundred tons, a total complement of one hundred and fifty men, and a cargo of cloth, coral, and washbasins. It was hardly surprising that the Indians greeted him with some contempt.

To this day, historians are unsure about Yung Lo's motives in sending forth his fleets. Was he simply attempting to enlarge and consolidate the imperial tributary system? Was he searching foreign courts for his deposed nephew, who was thought to have fled abroad? The eunuch admirals may have wanted to promote commerce, but to Chinese officials the Ming expeditions must have seemed an aberration. Confucian ideology embodied a contempt for both trade and barbarians that was understandable in a vast, self-sufficient, agrarian empire. It did not befit the Son of Heaven to send out an emissary — particularly if that emissary was drawn from that despised group, the eunuchs — to drum up trade and tributaries. Foreigners uninterested in becoming part of the penumbra of Chinese civilization could be ignored as long as they did not disturb the empire.

Upon Yung Lo's death in 1424, his successor was persuaded to cancel the expedition scheduled for that year. The swift demise of the new emperor gave Ming seafaring a final, glorious lease of life: in 1431–33 Cheng Ho led a seventh cruise, establishing relations with twenty more states from Java to East Africa. That voyage marked the end of China's great naval epoch, for the cost of the expeditions, coupled with the cost of constructing the new capital, had weakened the government's financial position. More significantly, the centuries-old menace from the steppe, this time taking the shape of a recrudescence of Mongol power, had forced the Ming to shift their attention from overseas to inner Asia.

It was a fateful shift, doubtless related to the earlier decision to move the capital from central China to Peking, where the emperor was perforce more sensitive to a threat from the north. Had Ming fleets continued to ply the eastern oceans after the death of Yung Lo,

they would have come into contact with the maritime nations of Europe at an earlier date, gaining from that contact an awareness of the civilization that was about to overtake China in science and technology. Toward the end of the Ming period, Jesuits were allowed to establish themselves in Peking, and men like Matthew Ricci imparted some of the advances made by astronomers and mathematicians in the West. But as Joseph Needham has demonstrated, the Chinese were far more knowledgeable about science than the Jesuits gave them credit for being, and their faith in the enduring superiority of their civilization was not shaken by their limited contact with scientific advances abroad. In a sense their faith was justified, for the civilization reestablished under the Ming and presided over by the Son of Heaven in the Forbidden City persisted for another five hundred years. But by turning inward in the fifteenth century, the Chinese ensured that when the awakening came, it would be more sudden and unpleasant than it might otherwise have been.

Perhaps after the traumatic experience of the Mongol conquest, the Chinese were not ready for a dialogue with another alien culture. Essentially the Ming era was a time of reaffirmation of traditional Chinese values; a time for the inculcation of accepted principles rather than the elaboration of new ideas; a time of orthodoxy, not exploration. In a sense the Ming maritime expeditions were an intellectual as well as historical aberration. Far more typical of the dynasty — and far more congenial to Confucian scholars and bureaucrats — was another great achievement of Yung Lo's reign, the compilation of the *Yung Lo Ta-tien,* the *Yung Lo Encyclopedia.* Prepared by some two thousand scholars over the course of three years, the encyclopedia reproduced or excerpted everything of value written during three millennia of Chinese cultural history. Though far too expensive to print — only three manuscript copies were ever made — the encyclopedia constituted a bench mark of Chinese civilization, one sufficiently massive to discourage all but the bravest intellectual adventurers.

It was the revival of one of the best features of Chinese civilization — the recruitment of a civil service on the basis of merit — that was heavily to blame for Ming orthodoxy, for as the examinations became increasingly formalized, rote learning of the Confucian classics became the best guarantee of success. Another potent reason for the lack of adventurousness of most Ming officials and scholars was that they had to tread warily under the often savage despotism of the Ming emperors. None of the later rulers attained the personal domination of Hung Wu and Yung Lo, but the situation remained uncertain and violence-ridden because the Forbidden City came under the control of the palace eunuchs, most of whom were drawn from the ranks of castrated criminals. A disgusted seventeenth-century Chinese scholar who had experienced thirty years of the Ming dynasty wrote:

> Throughout the Han, T'ang and Sung dynasties there was an endless series of disasters brought on by eunuchs, but none so frightful as those of the Ming. During the Han, T'ang and Sung there were eunuchs who interfered with the government, but no government which did whatever the eunuchs ordered [as the Ming did].

The eunuchs were not a force to be reckoned with in

The elderly gentleman holding a book at left and the philosopher seated beneath a cliff at right illustrate the contemplative mode of life enjoyed by Chinese scholars. Respect was not their only reward, however, for civil service personnel were recruited from among their ranks by means of public examinations. In a painting by the famed Ming artist Ch'iu Ying (below), candidates anxiously await the results of the competition.

The two groups that dominated the court of the Ming emperors are featured in artworks created during the period: Ch'iu Ying included two simpering eunuchs (left) in a painting; women playing a board game (right) and sewing (far right) decorate a pair of splendid porcelain vases.

the early years of the Ming dynasty. Hung Wu had tried to restrict their numbers to one hundred, had kept them illiterate, and had erected a tablet in his palace stating; "Eunuchs must have nothing to do with administration." Perhaps the tablet was left behind when Yung Lo moved the capital to Peking; certainly the growth of eunuch power and influence dates from his reign.

During the Ming dynasty, the staff of the imperial household consisted entirely of women and eunuchs. Under Hung Wu, women had dominated the palace, but by the time of Yung Lo's death in 1424 they ran only the Bureau of Apparel. Eunuchs were in charge of the bureaus of Palace Attendance, Ceremonies, Foodstuffs, Bedchamber, Handicrafts, and the Office of Staff Surveillance. By the end of the fifteenth century there were ten thousand eunuchs in the imperial service; toward the end of the sixteenth century it was not uncommon for more than three thousand to be recruited in a single year. By the end of the Ming era in 1644, there were some 70,000 eunuchs employed in the Forbidden City.

Yung Lo also set an important precedent for the use of eunuchs outside the palace by giving the command of his fleets to Cheng Ho. By 1644 there were an estimated 30,000 eunuchs performing administrative and military duties outside Peking. It was also Yung Lo who inaugurated a special cemetery for eunuchs and appointed a "patron saint" for them. The appalling manner in which the latter's beatification was achieved grimly illustrates the impact of Ming terror. Legend has it that Yung Lo once left a trusted general, Kang T'ieh, in charge of the Forbidden City while he was away on a hunting trip. Kang felt honored, but was fearful that his preferment would incite the jealousy of some rival. His qualms proved justified, for upon Yung Lo's return Kang T'ieh was accused of having taken liberties with the palace women. Kang then revealed that in anticipation of just such an accusation he had taken the precaution of castrating himself and concealing his scrotum in the emperor's saddle. The saddle was sent for and the story corroborated. An impressed Yung Lo made Kang his chief eunuch, and after the ex-general's death built a temple to him just outside the city wall. It was still serving as a refuge for eunuchs in the 1930's.

Eunuchs were the only male attendants allowed to live in the Forbidden City, and consequently they had unique access to the emperor. With few family interests to promote, they seemed more likely to be loyal to the emperor's interests — and as the Ming sovereigns progressively lost interest in governing, they allowed more and more power to accrue to the eunuchs, who were fitted neither by background, education, nor inclination to run a Confucian state. Under their influence, the Forbidden City became a hotbed of factionalism, intrigue, and vice.

The decadence of the Forbidden City, a major factor behind the decline of the Ming, produced a series of scandals during the last years of the dynasty. In 1615, a commoner penetrated the heir apparent's residence and assaulted eunuch attendants with a club before being arrested. Some bureaucrats who belonged to the Tung Lin faction (named after the famous academy in eastern China where they had studied) alleged that this attack had been inspired by the emperor himself in an

attempt to replace the heir apparent with the son of one of his favorite concubines, Mme. Cheng.

Despite the emperor's animosity, the heir apparent did succeed to the throne upon his father's death in 1620. A week later he became seriously ill, and it was rumored that Mme. Cheng, furious that her own son had been denied the throne and well aware of the new emperor's sexual appetite, had sent eight beautiful girls to him, certain that he would eventually fall ill from exhaustion. Mme. Cheng herself watched over the emperor's sickbed. She and Mme. Li, one of the new emperor's favorite concubines, prevented officials from seeing him and employed a eunuch physician whose potions seemed to make the emperor even sicker. After two weeks, during which anxious Tung Lin officials demanded the removal of Mme. Cheng and the punishment of the doctor, a delegation reached the emperor's bedside. The crisis seemed resolved. Then, two weeks later, the emperor, urged on by the women at his bedside, took some red pills prepared by a minor court official. Early the next morning he was dead.

Officials entering the Forbidden City to kowtow to the new emperor, a fifteen-year-old boy, found that Mme. Li was holding him in protective custody in the imperial residence hall and using eunuch guards to keep everyone away. Fortunately for the officials, who were again led by members of the Tung Lin faction, a sympathetic senior eunuch tricked Mme. Li into letting the young emperor go. Though she had lost her trump card, Mme. Li stubbornly announced that she would remain in the imperial residence hall and would peruse all official documents destined for the emperor. The threat of a third female usurpation of imperial power

— it had happened before under the Han and T'ang — horrified even Mme. Li's friends and relatives, who finally persuaded her to relinquish the residence hall.

The Tung Lin faction enjoyed but a brief triumph. With Mme. Li when she evacuated the residence hall was a fifty-two-year-old eunuch named Wei Chung-hsien. Despite his association with Mme. Li, Wei managed to ingratiate himself with the new emperor with the help of the latter's former nursemaid, Mme. K'o. The boy ruler, who was probably illiterate and had few interests beyond carpentry, allowed Wei Chung-hsien to become a virtual dictator. Members of the Tung Lin faction were disgraced, and some were arrested, tortured, and even executed. (The official history of the Ming states: "Those who were murdered are beyond calculation.") All memorials to the throne had to include lavish praise of the eunuch, and local officials erected temples in his honor. A proposal was even made that Wei Chung-hsien should rank with Confucius in ritual ceremonies, and the eunuch's nephew took the place of the emperor at a sacrificial ceremony in the imperial temple. The American Ming scholar Charles O. Hucker has commented that "it would appear probable that at no time in Chinese imperial history were court politics and ethics more debased."

Just when it seemed that the Forbidden City was to be the scene of the first eunuch usurpation in Chinese imperial history, the emperor died. Wei Chung-hsien was forced to commit suicide to avoid arrest, and his accomplice, Mme. K'o, was beaten to death. Ch'ung-chen, the new emperor, proved to be the last of the Ming line. By 1627, the year he ascended the throne, the regime was so demoralized that neither the new

In Chinese art, imitation is often the highest expression of admiration for past masters. Although refinement of traditional themes and styles was prized more than innovation during the Ming era, outstanding works of art were nonetheless produced. Exquisite detailing enlivens two Ming paintings (above and left) that depict conventional panoramas of pampered court ladies. A lacquered bamboo box (below) and an enameled double-gourd vase (left, above) are stunning examples of Ming craftsmanship.

emperor nor his officials were able to meet the grave challenges that faced them. The government was in a parlous financial condition, its treasury severely depleted by military expenditures incurred in the struggle against Manchu aggression on the northeast frontier. The Manchus, who derived from the same stock as the Jurchen founders of the Chin dynasty, had grown increasingly powerful under the great leader Nurhachi. Originally a Chinese tributary, Nurhachi threw off Chinese suzerainty and in 1616 set up a new Chin dynasty. Between 1618 and 1622 he conquered virtually all the Chinese-held territory in what later came to be known as Manchuria. The Ming desperately reinforced Shanhaikuan, the narrow pass between the mountains and the sea that would be the natural invasion route if the Manchus wished to attack Peking.

Defense against the Manchus cost the government 60,000,000 taels of silver in the period between 1618 and 1627, a third of which was incurred during the two and a half years of crisis between 1618 and 1620. The actual annual revenue during this period was only a putative 14,000,000 taels, of which only 70 per cent actually reached the central government. Despite this grave imbalance — and despite brave remonstrances from bureaucrats — successive emperors refused to curb their extravagance. Wan Li spent 90,000 taels on his marriage, 100,000 at the birth of a daughter, and some 12,000,000 taels on the investiture ceremonies of his various sons. He rebuilt burned-down buildings in the Forbidden City at a cost of over 9,000,000 taels for wood alone, while his grandson, T'ien-ch'i, whose reign witnessed three major fires, spent 6,000,000 taels on reconstruction. Official criticisms were leveled particularly at the lavishness of the Forbidden City's Court of Imperial Entertainments, which has been described as the "world's largest grocery store and dining hall" then in existence. As early as 1425, the hall is known to have employed 6,300 cooks to cater meals for an estimated 10,000 to 15,000 people a day. Rather than cut back on such expenditures the emperors preferred to send out eunuch tax commissioners to collect a wide range of emergency taxes. These measures may have increased tax revenue up to forty per cent, but they increased discontent proportionately.

The location of the capital also posed familiar economic problems during this period. Because of pirates, Yung Lo had abandoned the transportation of tax grain by sea in 1415. To supply the capital, he put the Grand Canal back into service by reopening the Yüan channel across west Shantung (see map, page 60). The imperial granaries in Peking received as much as 360,000 tons of grain a year by this route, but the cost of transportation was immense — about twice the cost of the grain itself — and the boats took up to a year to make the round trip. Throughout the Ming period, officials argued for the reopening of the sea route, but it was not until 1643 that a small experimental shipment was dispatched along the coast. It arrived within a month, and plans were made to send as much as half the tax grain by sea the following year — but by then the Ming had been overthrown.

Ironically, the downfall of the Ming dynasty was partially attributable to a major but misguided economy measure adopted shortly after the last emperor came to the throne. In 1629 he agreed to the abolition of the imperial postal service, a kind of pony express

that from Yüan times kept the Forbidden City in touch with the far reaches of the empire. Its abolition was to undermine central control and spark rebellions. In North China, ravaged by famines in the 1630's and 1640's, unemployed postal carriers became the core of bandit and rebel groups. Among their number was a quarrelsome young man named Li Tzu-ch'eng, a superb horseman and archer who joined his uncle's robber band in 1631 at the age of about twenty-six. On the death of his uncle five years later, Li, nicknamed the "Dashing King," extended his power into central China. In 1643 he set up a capital in Hupeh, and in the following year he issued coins to mark the official start of his reign.

On April 23, 1644, Li Tzu-ch'eng surrounded Peking. The emperor had earlier sent urgent appeals for help to Wu San-kuei, the thirty-two-year-old "Earl Who Pacifies the West," commander of the Shanhaikuan defenses. It was now quite clear that Wu could not arrive in time, but the emperor rejected Li's surrender proposals and climbed Coal Hill to contemplate the fate of his dynasty and its magnificent capital. On April 25, as Li attacked, the emperor rang the bell to summon his ministers. None appeared, and the emperor returned to Coal Hill, where he is said to have committed suicide by hanging himself from a tree. His last message attributed the disaster that had befallen the Ming to bad advisers. On the same day, Li Tzu-ch'eng took the capital and ordered the bodies of the emperor and his chief consort to be put into rough coffins and deposited outside the gates of the Forbidden City.

Wu San-kuei was torn by conflicting emotions. He would probably have surrendered to save the life of his father, whom Li Tzu-ch'eng was holding prisoner in Peking, if he had not received news that Li had also seized his favorite concubine, "Round-faced Beauty." Instead of surrendering, he vowed revenge. Wu came to terms with the Manchus, opened Shanhaikuan Pass to them, and together they defeated Li Tzu-ch'eng's advancing forces at the end of May. Li retreated to the capital, where he melted down all the silver in the Forbidden City and, early in June, proclaimed himself emperor in the Hall of Military Prowess. On June 3, Li burned part of the Forbidden City and the towers of the nine city gates. Then, after overseeing the execution of Wu San-kuei's father and family, he evacuated the capital. Two days later the Manchu forces entered Peking. The mandate of heaven had descended yet again upon an alien dynasty.

V

The Curse of the Yehe Woman

Wu San-kuei served the Manchus well for thirty years before he rose in revolt. During those years he played a key role in the final defeat of the Ming, leading an expedition into Burma to capture the last pretender, whom he brought back to China and executed. Richly rewarded for his services, Wu became a virtually independent satrap ruling Southwest China. All this was altered in 1673, when the second Manchu emperor, K'ang-hsi — who was forceful and determined beyond his nineteen years — decided to impose imperial control throughout China. Wu and other regional overlords rebelled. At first Wu asserted that he wished to restore the previous dynasty — which must have raised a hollow laugh among any remaining Ming loyalists — but early in 1678 he proclaimed himself the first emperor of a new dynasty. Fortunately for K'ang-hsi, the aging rebel died less than six months later and although Wu's grandson continued to fight, the "revolt of the three feudatories" was extinguished by 1681. The Ch'ing, or "Pure," dynasty of the Manchus was now firmly in control of all China.

Imitating their barbarian predecessors, the Manchus took steps to prevent their own assimilation by the Chinese, who outnumbered them almost fifty to one. Even before the conquest of China proper, a Manchu ruler called together a solemn assembly of notables to hear a rereading of the famous Chin decree that forbade Mongols to adopt either Chinese names or attire. The Manchu ruler warned his countrymen that the Chin had collapsed because they had not heeded the decree and had allowed their martial qualities to be sapped by easy living.

After the conquest, Manchus were forbidden to intermarry with the Chinese or to adopt such Chinese customs as foot-binding. Chinese subjects were forced to shave their heads and wear Manchu-style pigtails. Special efforts were made to keep the Manchu language, religion, and clan system alive. In Manchuria, Chinese immigration into the central and northern areas was forbidden in the hope of preserving inviolate the wellspring of the Manchu way of life; the "willow palisade" — a deep ditch lined with willows that had been dug by the Ming to keep out barbarian tribesmen — now served to hem in the Chinese. After serious communal riots in Peking in 1648, virtually all Chinese residents were compelled to move into the outer city and this area became known as the Chinese City. At the same time, the Manchus arrogated almost exclusive occupancy of the inner city to themselves, and that area became known as the Tatar City. In the government, top Chinese officials were duplicated man for man by Manchus who worked alongside them and kept an eye on them. The central armed forces, on which Ch'ing control ultimately depended, were restricted to Manchus, Mongols, and anti-Ming Chinese.

Had the Manchus sought to preserve their power only by traditional methods, they would have been no more successful than the Mongols. Instead, they managed to establish one of the greatest and most long-lived of Chinese dynasties. K'ang-hsi's achievement was to win over the Confucian elite, a task at which Kublai had so signally failed. He did this by preserving the examination system for the recruitment of bureaucrats, and also by encouraging traditional scholarship on the gargantuan scale laid down by Yung Lo. The encyclopedia that K'ang-hsi sponsored — entitled *A Collection*

of Books and Illustrations of Ancient and Modern Times — comprised 5,000 volumes, 10,000 chapters, and roughly 100,000,000 ideograms. Although it was not as large as Yung Lo's, it was at least printed. When K'ang-hsi toured the old Ming strongholds of central China, he publicized his personal devotion to classical Chinese studies. He also cultivated the image of the traditional imperial father figure by inquiring benevolently about the well-being of the people and the state of the harvest wherever he went.

But the Manchus' success was attributable to more than just good public relations. Of the four great barbarian conquerors who ruled from Peking, the Manchus were the best suited to govern the bureaucratic Chinese state. They were the least nomadic of the four, inhabiting walled towns and engaging in a more advanced type of agriculture than that of their Jurchen forebears. They had long lived cheek-by-jowl with the Chinese way of life and had adapted to its patterns. As they extended their hold over southern Manchuria during the decades before their capture of Peking, the Manchus gained valuable experience in employing Chinese bureaucrats to run a Chinese-style administration for them.

In short, the Manchus accepted the fact that their frontier state was part of the Chinese world. Wu San-kuei, who was a native of southern Manchuria, understood all this, and it was probably his sense of rapport with the Manchus as much as his love for the Round-faced Beauty that led him to open Shanhaikuan Pass to them. After their victory the Manchus showed that, unlike the Mongols, they did not think of themselves as foreign conquerors. The first Ch'ing emperor

proclaimed that he had elevated his old state "to receive the new mandate." His successor, K'ang-hsi, issued an imperial edict of sixteen maxims that instructed his subjects, Confucian-style, in the correct norms of conduct.

The success of the Ch'ing dynasty meant that henceforth the barbarians who lived north of the Great Wall need not be thought of as antagonists to be suppressed or appeased, but could be considered legitimate components of the Chinese world. Appropriately, it was under the Ch'ing that Inner and Outer Mongolia, Chinese Turkistan (modern Sinkiang), and Tibet were all fully incorporated into the Chinese empire, whose boundaries stretched even beyond those of the T'ang empire ruled by Hsuan Tsung. The Chinese began to regard the lands beyond the wall as part of China proper; the frontier had become part of the empire.

Peking, essentially a frontier city, was a more fitting capital of this new Chinese imperium than it had ever been before. It was also ideally located, roughly equidistant between the Manchus' ancestral home and the Yangtze rice bowl. Fortunately, Li Tzu-ch'eng had not leveled the city, and the Ch'ing had only to reconstruct some buildings and restore others. The major palaces of the Forbidden City that the modern visitor sees today are almost exclusively Ch'ing reconstructions of Ming originals.

The first step taken by the Ch'ing to make Peking their own capital was to give new names to the three major halls of state in the Forbidden City. In 1645, only a year after the capture of Peking, they were renamed the T'ai Ho Tien, Chung Ho Tien, and Pao

Ho Tien, the halls of Supreme, Central, and Protecting Harmony. The Ch'ing thus introduced one of the central Confucian concepts into the names of the most important buildings in the empire. As the classic Confucian work, *The Mean,* states:

> When the passions, such as pleasure and anger and sorrow and joy have not awakened, the state is called that of centrality. When these passions awaken and each and all attain due measure and degree, it is called the state of harmony. The state of centrality is the great root and the state of harmony is the far-reaching Way of all existence in the world. Once centrality and harmony are realized, Heaven and earth take their proper places and all things receive their full nourishment.

This symbolic appeal for harmony was perhaps a calculated piece of psychological warfare, issued as it was by an alien dynasty that was then still engaged in conquering the Middle Kingdom by the sword.

At the time of the renaming of the Hall of Supreme Harmony in 1645 major repairs were made to the structure. Another reconstruction was ordered by K'ang-hsi in 1669, but that work was not completed until thirty years later. In 1765, under K'ang-hsi's grandson, Ch'ien Lung, all three major halls on the Dragon Pavement were repaired. In 1797, two years after Ch'ien Lung abdicated for reasons of ancestral piety — he did not want to reign longer than his illustrious grandfather — the three great private halls of the Inner Court were destroyed by fire and had to be completely rebuilt.

Such disastrous conflagrations were not uncommon within the Forbidden City, where the major building material was wood. To this day, no one knows why Chinese builders did not use stone for their palaces. They certainly knew how to use the material, for they built walls and bridges, pagodas and tombs with it. Perhaps the most convincing explanation, offered by Professor Arthur Wright, is that the Chinese imperial tradition, unlike the Roman, did not originate in the expansion of the city-state. The city was not, therefore, a unit to be immortalized in stone; the concept of *urbs aeterna* was totally alien. Moreover, by the time the Sui and T'ang set about constructing Ch'ang-an even the idea of an eternal dynasty, espoused by Ch'in Shih Huang Ti when he first united the empire, had been exposed as illusory; the concept of the dynastic cycle had been established in its place. Although the Ming and Ch'ing emperors demanded lasting stone mausoleums, they were well aware that their memories would be preserved in the written words of the dynastic history rather than in architectural monuments.

Another cultural factor may have been the Chinese concern with the affairs of this world rather than salvation in the next. Certainly in Europe and India religion encouraged the construction of monumental and enduring cathedrals and temples, conceivable only in stone. It is significant that the few surviving buildings of T'ang Ch'ang-an are Buddhist temples like the Great Wild Goose Pagoda, the monument of an alien creed.

The dominant architectural feature of the great halls and palaces of the Forbidden City is the traditional Chinese curved roof. The curved line was made possible by the use of a roof support system more flexible than the rigid, triangulated truss employed in

Jesuits were welcome at the court of K'ang-hsi. As a child, the heir to the Manchu throne was tutored by a missionary; as an adult, the emperor commissioned Father Matteo Ripa to engrave a series of views (above and right) of the summer palace at Jehol, which was situated north of the Great Wall.

Europe. The Chinese used a beam frame system in which progressively shorter crossbeams, separated by struts, supported longitudinal beams known as purlins. The rafters of the roof rested on the purlins. By varying the relative lengths of the crossbeams and thus the position of the purlins, curved roofs could be produced from short, straight rafters.

The Chinese beam support system could just as easily have been used to build straight roofs, and the British architect Andrew Boyd, who asserts that "structure does not dictate architectural form," attributes the curved roof to aesthetic choice. That great popularizer of Chinese culture Lin Yutang points out that one of the basic tenets of Chinese calligraphy is the "interplay of rigid straight lines and curving forms," and he suggests that in the Peking palaces the curving roofs form a harmonious whole with the straight lines of the base and pillars, producing a combination of grace and strength.

The other striking feature of the Forbidden City is the unabashed use of color, which serves to differentiate the three principal architectural elements of the buildings. The terraces — the podiums upon which Chinese buildings have been placed since time immemorial to elevate them above the damp earth — are a brilliant white. The wooden pillars that support the roofs are a dull red, a reminder that Chinese builders were using mercuric oxide as a preservative on building timber as far back as the eleventh century B.C. The walls — which are not supports but only screens — are red too. The roofs are tiled in imperial sun yellow. Together, as seen from the terrace of the Meridian Gate or from Coal Hill, the roofs form a billowing

golden sea, for the Forbidden City is not one great palace with outbuildings, such as one finds in Europe, but a veritable city — a 250-acre complex of some seventy-five halls, palaces, temples, pavilions, libraries, and studios, linked or separated by numerous courtyards, gardens, gates, and walls, the whole balanced athwart the great north-south axis of the capital.

The Ch'ing did not restrict themselves to rebuilding the palaces of the Forbidden City. Alongside the lakes to the west of the palace complex, lakes that the Ming had extended southward and divided into the Pei Hai, Chung Hai, and Nan Hai — the North, Middle, and South seas — the Ch'ing built busily and extensively throughout the dynasty. They left behind over a hundred residences, reception halls, temples, theaters, libraries, and summer houses. In 1651, on the Island of Flowered Jade in the Pei Hai, the first Ch'ing emperor built the White Pagoda (or Dagoba, as it is usually called, because of its Indian lines) to mark the first visit of a dalai lama to Peking. It was erected on the site of the Hall of the Moon — probably Kublai's first residence in Ta-tu — which had collapsed in the sixteenth century. The White Pagoda reminded Osvald Sirén, the historian of Peking's palaces, of "a gigantic bottle with a wide body and a long neck ending in an ornamental plug." It remains a dominating feature of the Peking skyline to this day.

Seven miles to the northwest of the city, in an area where the Chin, Yüan, and Ming had all built pleasure palaces, K'ang-hsi began what was to become, under Ch'ien Lung, the great Ch'ing Summer Palace. Three quarters of the square-mile park was occupied by the K'un Ming Lake, the rest by Longevity Hill. The park

was dotted with palaces, including some Italianate ones designed by Jesuit missionaries. The forty "most beautiful views" of the park were painted by two famous artists and published with poems by Ch'ien Lung.

Two days' journey north of Peking, in what had been the hilly homeland of the Khitan Liao, K'ang-hsi started construction of another great summer palace in 1703. Here in Jehol, K'ang-hsi conducted the great hunts that were one of his devices to prevent the Manchus from going soft. The loveliest views of this palace were painted by a Chinese and engraved by the priest Matteo Ripa.

In 1793, the British diplomat Lord Macartney came to Jehol to petition Ch'ien Lung for better trading opportunities and the establishment of diplomatic relations. Macartney was a skilled diplomat who had negotiated with the autocratic Catherine the Great of Russia and some of the wilier Indian maharajahs, but his expertise proved of no avail with Ch'ien Lung. The emperor received Macartney affably despite the latter's refusal to perform the tributary kowtow, and Macartney was suitably impressed with the beauties of the summer palace. But there was a basic problem that Macartney could not overcome, namely the Chinese lack of interest in foreign countries and their products. As Ch'ien Lung said in a famous edict he approved at Jehol for Macartney to take back to George III:

Now you, O King, have presented various objects to the throne, and mindful of your loyalty in presenting offerings from afar, we have specially ordered the Yamen to receive them. . . . Nevertheless we have never valued ingenious articles, nor do we have the slightest need of your country's manufactures. . . .

You, O King, should simply act in conformity with our wishes by strengthening your loyalty and swearing perpetual obedience so as to ensure that your country may share the blessings of peace.

Ch'ien Lung's lofty self-confidence was founded not only upon the traditional Chinese belief that their empire was the center of the civilized world, but also upon China's current power and prosperity. The country's population of some 300,000,000 was larger than that of any other contemporary state, and although China had undergone no industrial revolution, its agriculture, irrigation, water transportation, and handicrafts were highly developed. Economically, the country was self-sufficient; Ch'ien Lung was correct in thinking that he had no need for foreign goods. Politically, China was a model of stability and good government; between them, K'ang-hsi and Ch'ien Lung ruled China for 120 years, and the country was thus provided with excellent leadership for most of the first century and a half of Ch'ing rule.

In the eighteenth century the Middle Kingdom was indeed the most impressive state in the world, and its philosophy, institutions, and rulers were much admired by such European thinkers as Voltaire and Montesquieu, who learned about China from the writings of the Jesuits. And yet that percipient observer, Lord Macartney, sensed that all was not well:

The Empire of China is an old, crazy First rate man-of-war, which a fortunate succession of able and vigilant officers has contrived to keep afloat for these one hundred and fifty years past, and to overawe their neighbours merely by her bulk and appearance, but whenever an insufficient man happens to have the

Artworks created during Ch'ien Lung's long reign reveal a bemused curiosity about the West. A dazzling scroll (left) depicts the emperor — in a dragon-drawn celestial carriage — awaiting tribute from Portuguese ambassadors; on a unique revolving brushpot (far left), made for palace use, Europeans cross a bridge to reach Ch'ien Lung. The foreign factories at the port of Canton appear on a painted fan (below), and carved wood-and-ivory "barbarians" hold aloft the Buddhist lotus (left) and umbrella (right).

command upon deck, adieu to the discipline and safety of the ship. She may perhaps not sink outright; she may drift some time as a wreck, and will then be dashed to pieces on the shore; but she can never be rebuilt on the old bottom.

The nineteenth century witnessed the fulfillment of Lord Macartney's prophecy.

During the early decades of that century, the Europeans seemed but another group of troublesome barbarians. Then came China's first big defeat, at the hands of the British, in the Opium War of 1839–42. When the British threatened the capital's future grain supplies by seizing part of the Grand Canal in 1842, the emperor quickly came to terms. The Ch'ing signed China's first commercial treaty — which was what Macartney had asked for fifty years earlier. Much of the war had been fought near Canton, more than a thousand miles south of the capital, and the court had remained frozen in its complacent isolationism. Only after the British and the French had taken Peking and sacked the Summer Palace in the hostilities of 1856–60 were the first belated measures taken to strengthen the country's defenses. At the same time, China took a further step into the modern world, conceding another of Macartney's requests — the stationing of diplomatic representatives at the capital. In the last decades of the century, a legation quarter grew up just south of the Imperial City.

At mid-century the Chinese, as good Confucians, would readily have admitted that their defeats were attributable to the leadership of what Macartney called "insufficient men." But the emergence of first-rate leaders in Peking and the provinces — and the sup-

pression of the massive Taiping Rebellion of 1850–64 — inspired the dynasty with the confidence that it could renew itself by grafting Western technology onto Chinese institutions. This illusion was finally shattered by the hitherto despised Japanese "dwarfs," who defeated the Chinese in the Sino-Japanese War of 1894–95 and forced them to cede Formosa and suzerainty over Korea.

This traumatic shock gave the more radical reformers their chance. In January 1898 their leader, K'ang Yu-wei, confronted the pillars of the Confucian establishment. The Manchu general Jung-lu stated: "The institutions of the ancestors cannot be changed." K'ang replied: "We cannot preserve the realm of the ancestors; what is the use of their institutions?" Li Hung-chang (the most prestigious Chinese official of the day) asked: "Shall we abolish all the Six Boards and throw away all the existing institutions and rules?" And K'ang replied: "The laws and governmental system . . . have made China weak and will ruin her. Undoubtedly they should be done away with."

For a hundred days, K'ang and his supporters gained the ear of the twenty-seven-year-old emperor, Kuang Hsü. Between June 11 and September 21, 1898, some forty radical reform edicts were issued from the Forbidden City to a thunderstruck empire. But K'ang Yu-wei had not convinced Jung-lu, Li Hung-chang, and the Confucian establishment of the rightness of his policies. They still did not accept K'ang's argument that the Confucian state, with its agrarian base and its static social structure, was unsuited to the modern world — that it could never, as Macartney foresaw, be "rebuilt on the old bottom," but would have to be

Less than fifty years after Ch'ien Lung received England's first ambassador to China, the two nations were at arms. Sparked by British refusal to halt the illegal traffic in opium — the debilitating effects of which are dramatized below — the Opium War of 1839–42 ended with China's humiliating defeat. A British participant in the naval assault of Chinkiang, a major episode in that war, drew the sketch at left. China's mid-century woes were not over with the signing of the peace treaty, however, for the popularly supported Taiping Rebellion soon posed a serious threat to imperial authority. A detail from a Ch'ing painting (overleaf) shows government forces attacking a Taiping stronghold.

replaced through a fundamental social and industrial revolution. In its hour of need, the Confucian establishment turned to the sixty-four-year-old empress dowager, Tz'u Hsi, who was living in semiretirement at the Summer Palace and indulging her passion for picnics and amateur theatricals.

Tz'u Hsi had been a concubine of Hsien Fêng, who reigned from 1851 to 1861. As such, she was the first woman of the Yehe clan to be taken into the imperial harem in well over two hundred years. In 1619 her ancestor, Prince Gintaisi, had died fighting Nurhachi in the last great struggle before the latter united all the Manchu tribes. At his death Gintaisi had cursed his conquerors, prophesying that Nurhachi's line and the whole Manchu race would one day perish at the hands of a woman of the Yehe clan. From then on, the superstitious Manchu rulers forswore Yehe concubines. But by 1852, when Tz'u Hsi entered the imperial harem at the age of seventeen, the memory of the curse had presumably faded. It was an unfortunate lapse.

In 1856, Tz'u Hsi consolidated her position in the imperial household by bearing the emperor his only son. When the emperor died in 1861 at Jehol — whence he had fled from the Anglo-French forces — twenty-six-year-old Tz'u Hsi gave the Chinese a first glimpse of her iron nerve and her gift for political intrigue. She outwitted three powerful courtiers in the struggle for the regency during the minority of her son, T'ung Chih. And when her son died in 1875 from a combination of smallpox and syphilis, Tz'u Hsi struck again. She insisted on the immediate choice of a successor, knowing that if her pregnant daughter-in-law, with whom she was on bad terms, produced a son, it would

spell the end of her power. Tz'u Hsi engineered the selection of an infant nephew, the son of her favorite sister, and so retained her regency.

In 1889, after she had arranged the marriage of the young emperor, Kuang Hsü, to a niece she could trust, Tz'u Hsi relinquished control of daily administration. To signal her retirement, she moved her official residence within the Forbidden City from the Palace of Peace and Tranquillity to the Palace of Peaceful Old Age, where Ch'ien Lung had lived after his abdication. She spent most of her semiretirement at the Summer Palace, which she partially repaired with monies earmarked for the Chinese navy. It was symbolic of the isolationist outlook of the Ch'ing dynasty that although China was being threatened by seafaring barbarians, navy funds were diverted to satisfy the demands of the self-indulgent empress dowager. Tz'u Hsi's comfort cost the country dearly: the Japanese won their decisive victories in the war of 1894–95 at sea.

Tz'u Hsi kept in touch with affairs of state even in retirement, and she soon learned of the opposition to Kuang Hsü's reform policies. The emperor and his advisers, who were well aware that the empress dowager would be a formidable opponent if she heeded the appeals of their adversaries, decided to place her under house arrest. Before doing so they would have to kill Jung-lu, who had been Tz'u Hsi's confidant since childhood and was in command of troops in North China.

The emperor knew he could not activate such a plot from the Summer Palace, where every eunuch was his aunt's spy, and in September he returned to the Forbidden City. There, in a secret interview in the Palace of Heavenly Purity, he entrusted the murder of Jung-lu

Tz'u Hsi's favorite residence was the rebuilt Summer Palace below the Western Hills, about seven miles northwest of the capital. There, amid priceless treasures such as the nephrite vase at right, she periodically withdrew from the pressures of Peking. The tranquillity of her vast pleasure ground was enhanced by "outings" on the two-story, eighty-foot-long marble "boat" (left) that stands stationary in the nearby lake.

to Yüan Shih-k'ai, a Chinese general supposedly loyal to the emperor. Yüan betrayed the plot to Jung-lu, who immediately left his Tientsin headquarters to brief the empress dowager. Tz'u Hsi then summoned a conference of top conservative officials at the Summer Palace, and at their request she agreed to resume power. Jung-lu was ordered to replace the guards in the Forbidden City with his own men, and then to return to Tientsin. The conclave ended toward midnight.

The following morning, September 21, 1898, the emperor spent some time in the Hall of Central Harmony on the Dragon Pavement studying the prayers he planned to recite at the autumnal sacrifice to the tutelary deities. He never performed that ceremony, for as he left the hall he was arrested by Jung-lu's men and escorted to an island in the Nan Hai known as the Ocean Terrace — precisely where K'ang Yu-wei had suggested confining the empress dowager. There Kuang Hsü was visited by his dreaded aunt, who told him that she would allow him to live and to retain his imperial title but that he would henceforth be under constant watch. She denounced him for working with Chinese traitors to the Manchu dynasty, and when Kuang Hsü's favorite consort, the Pearl Concubine, pleaded on her knees on behalf of the emperor, Tz'u Hsi ordered her confined to another part of the Forbidden City. The only consort allowed near Kuang Hsü was Tz'u Hsi's niece, the empress, whom he hated.

The empress dowager executed as many of the reforming officials as she could lay her hands on, and she repealed most of their measures. Her new advisers included some of the most reactionary and ill-informed Manchu princes of the court. Under their influence

she was persuaded to pursue a dangerous policy of renewed confrontation with the imperialist powers, although China was little better prepared for such a struggle than it had been at the time of the Opium War.

The agents of Tz'u Hsi's growing xenophobia were the members of the Society of the Righteous and Harmonious Fists, known to Westerners as the Boxers. The Boxer movement emerged in North China in 1898 as an expression of peasant unrest at a time of economic distress and political uncertainty. It was antiforeign because some of the country's ills could be traced to the imperialists, while others could be foisted on them. The Boxers' particular targets were the missionaries and their Chinese converts.

The Western missionaries who had followed their countries' flags into China in the nineteenth century had been associated with some of the worst aspects of imperialism. In the 1830's, boats that carried opium also passed out religious tracts, and missionaries, like Western businessmen, acquired special privileges. Two centuries earlier, before their order was suppressed by the pope, the Jesuits had tried to convert China from the top down, striving with some success to make Christian dogmas and practices blend with the Confucian ideas of the bureaucratic elite. But in the nineteenth century, both Catholic and Protestant missionaries aimed at converting the uneducated masses, and aroused resentment by preventing their flocks from maintaining customs inimical to Christianity.

The Boxers themselves espoused an amorphous amalgam of magical Taoism and Buddhism that supposedly made them invulnerable to bullets. In early 1900 they stepped up their attacks on missionaries and

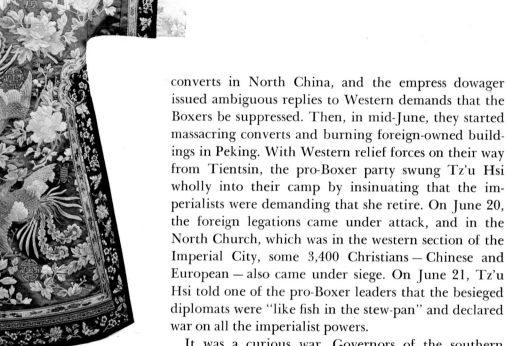

converts in North China, and the empress dowager
issued ambiguous replies to Western demands that the
Boxers be suppressed. Then, in mid-June, they started
massacring converts and burning foreign-owned buildings in Peking. With Western relief forces on their way
from Tientsin, the pro-Boxer party swung Tz'u Hsi
wholly into their camp by insinuating that the imperialists were demanding that she retire. On June 20,
the foreign legations came under attack, and in the
North Church, which was in the western section of the
Imperial City, some 3,400 Christians — Chinese and
European — also came under siege. On June 21, Tz'u
Hsi told one of the pro-Boxer leaders that the besieged
diplomats were "like fish in the stew-pan" and declared
war on all the imperialist powers.

It was a curious war. Governors of the southern
provinces, convinced of the folly of it all, concocted the
fiction that the declaration did not have the empress
dowager's full authorization, and they continued to
maintain cordial relations with local foreign forces.
Even Tz'u Hsi's faithful supporter Jung-lu regarded the
siege as "worse than an outrage, it is a piece of stupidity
which will be remembered against China for all time."
Knowing that the imperialist powers would exact a
fearful vengeance if the diplomats were slaughtered,
Jung-lu failed to prosecute the siege vigorously, using
his artillery very sparingly. Even the empress dowager
wavered briefly: she permitted a truce to be arranged
toward the end of the first month of the siege, during
which she sent the beleaguered diplomats two cart-
loads of melons, vegetables, ice, and flour.

The indecisiveness of the Chinese attack permitted
both the legations and the North Church to hold out

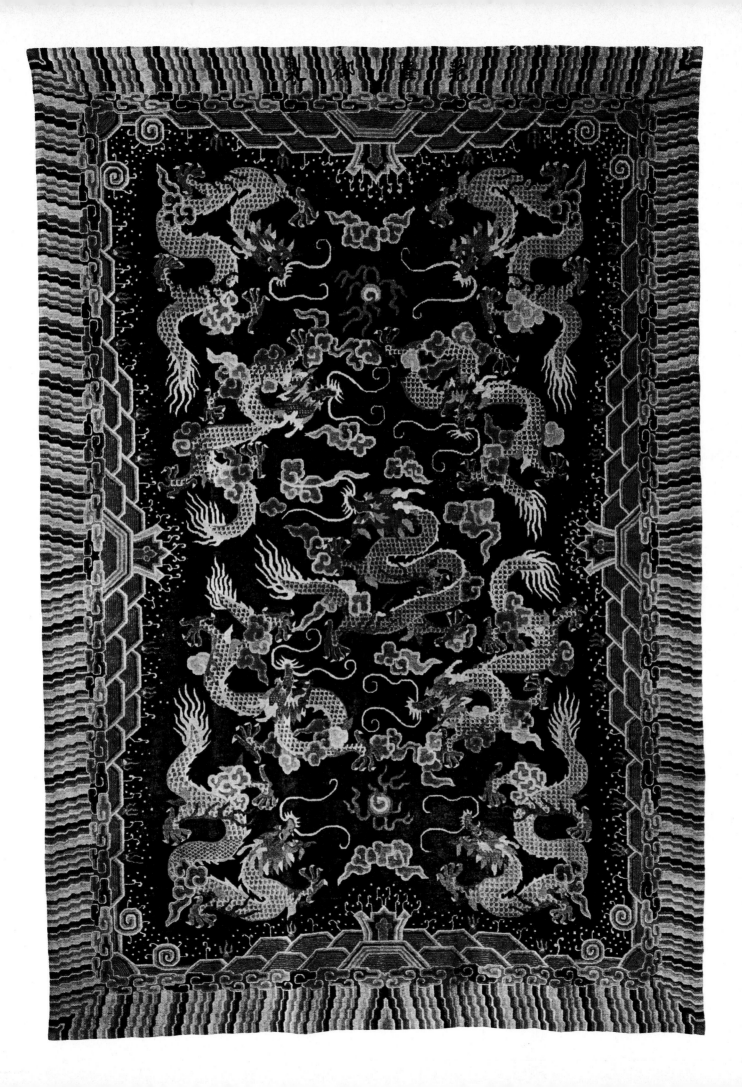

Pawns in the game of economic imperialism, the Chinese people endured decades of humiliation and exploitation before rising in rebellion against the colonial powers that had partitioned their country into spheres of influence in the mid-1800's. By the turn of the century, public pilloryings (left and near right) and preemptory executions (middle right) had become commonplace — and in 1900 they touched off an intensely xenophobic and apparently spontaneous uprising, the Boxer Rebellion. That quixotic and ill-fated insurrection quickly turned into a bloodbath for its fomentors, whose corpses litter the rampart at far right.

with surprisingly little loss of life. The vanguard of the allied relief column arrived on August 14. Within the Forbidden City, the Grand Council was in almost continuous session in the Palace of Peaceful Old Age, and at about 4 P.M. a nobleman burst unceremoniously into the audience hall and announced: "Old Buddha [as Tz'u Hsi was familiarly known], the foreign devils have come." The next messenger brought news that Indian troops were encamped in the Temple of Heaven. Shortly before midnight, Tz'u Hsi summoned the Grand Council yet again, this time to the Hall of Imperial Supremacy, her normal audience hall in the northeast section of the Forbidden City (see diagram, page 73). Like the last Ming emperor, she found that almost everyone had already deserted her. But Tz'u Hsi was made of sterner stuff than Ming Ch'ung-chen. She had no intention of committing suicide. She coolly made arrangements to escape with the emperor early the following morning, and then retired briefly to her apartments in the small pavilion known as the Hall of the Cultivation of Character.

At 3 A.M. on August 15, after only an hour's rest, Tz'u Hsi rose and hurriedly disguised herself in peasant dress. Outside, the emperor's concubines were waiting to bid farewell. The Pearl Concubine pleaded that the emperor be allowed to remain behind, or that she be permitted to accompany him on his flight. This infuriated Tz'u Hsi, who had the hapless consort thrown down a nearby well. Then she and the emperor hid themselves in country carts and rattled out of the Gate of Divine Military Genius, the main north gateway, escorted by the chief eunuch. It was certainly an ignominious exit from the Forbidden City, which was

now left to the mercy of men the Chinese had long called foreign devils.

At 7 A.M. on the same day, the commander of the American detachment of the relief column, without consulting his allies, ordered his troops to take the Imperial City. The plan of attack was simple: some artillery pieces were mounted in the tower of the Ch'ien Men to give cover, and the infantry advanced northward along the city's central axis. With the help of battering rams, gates were forced and eventually the wall of the Imperial City was scaled. Pausing just long enough to raise the American flag on the ramparts, the attackers continued on toward the Forbidden City, forcing their way through the Gate of Heavenly Peace and the Gate of Correct Deportment. They were about to attack the Meridian Gate, the entrance to the Forbidden City itself, when they were suddenly ordered to withdraw. The Russian and French commanders had convinced their colleagues that the American drive must be halted because desecration of the Forbidden City would cause irreparable damage to relations between the imperialist powers and China. All that the whole futile exercise had achieved was to prove that the massive fortifications of Ming-Ch'ing Peking were still formidable military obstacles, even in the age of modern artillery.

The Forbidden City had been saved from physical destruction, but it was not to be protected from looters. There was a triumphal march of allied forces through the Forbidden City on August 28, a march designed to prevent the birth of a legend that some supernatural force had stopped the allies from entering its precincts. After the parade, diplomats and officers were shown

around the Forbidden City by eunuchs — and they reportedly carried off anything that caught their fancy. Their depredations did not end there. German detachments were sent out on punitive and plundering expeditions and the allied commander in chief, Field Marshal Count von Waldersee — who was furious at the unfavorable publicity these sorties got in the London *Times* — consoled himself in the arms of a Chinese prostitute on one of the imperial beds. The French helped despoil the Imperial Observatory of instruments presented to the Ch'ing by Louis XIV. The Russians looted the Summer Palace, where Tz'u Hsi's throne was thrown into the lake and "lewd and ribald drawings and writings" were scrawled on her bedroom walls.

Tz'u Hsi had the last laugh, however, for with typical thoroughness she had ordered the greatest treasures of the Forbidden City buried under the courtyard of the Palace of Peaceful Old Age, whence they were recovered upon her return. That was not to be for seventeen months, however, during which Tz'u Hsi made her headquarters at Sian, the modern city on the site of Ch'ang-an and the scene of the worst Boxer massacres. Here she dined comfortably using the gold-and-silver place settings acquired for one of Ch'ien Lung's tours. Her expenditure on food — a mere $60 a day — was a tenth of what she was accustomed to spending in the Forbidden City.

There was much talk of establishing a new capital, either at Sian or farther west. But Tz'u Hsi was too old to forsake the pleasures of her beloved Summer Palace, even if it had been defiled. After all, this flight and the one she had made to Jehol with her husband forty years earlier were the only occasions on which she had left the environs of Peking. As soon as it became clear that great power rivalry would enable her to return to Peking and resume her former position of unchallenged supremacy, all talk of moving the capital abruptly ended.

In late October 1901, Tz'u Hsi began a long, stately, almost triumphant return home. She covered the last section of the journey by train, the first such trip by a Chinese ruler, and she arrived in Peking on January 6, 1902. At the station she made a special effort to display amiability toward the foreigners who had gathered to watch her arrival — and in the weeks and months ahead she was to consolidate this smiling image by holding many receptions for foreign ladies, who were purportedly captivated by the empress dowager's considerable charm.

But of course not even as strong-willed a ruler as Tz'u Hsi could pretend that nothing had changed except her attitude toward Europeans. The Boxer uprising dealt the final blow to Chinese hopes for dealing with the West by traditional means. Fundamental reform was now acknowledged to be essential by the empress dowager herself, and she was prepared to sanction measures more radical than those for which Kuang Hsü had been supplanted only five years earlier. A mortal blow was dealt to the Confucian system by the abolition of the traditional civil service examinations, and the emissaries sent abroad by Tz'u Hsi to study Western government came back advocating constitutional monarchy.

The autocratic Tz'u Hsi was spared that indignity, however, for she died on November 15, 1908. By a

coincidence universally attributed to her characteristic vindictiveness, her nephew Kuang Hsü had died one day earlier. Yet another small child, the boy-emperor P'u-yi, succeeded to the throne.

Strangely, Tz'u Hsi's dying words contradicted her whole life, for she adjured her attendants:

> Never again allow any woman to hold the supreme power in the state. It is against the house-law of our Dynasty and should be strictly forbidden. Be careful not to permit eunuchs to meddle in Government matters. The Ming dynasty was brought to ruin by eunuchs, and its fate should be a warning to my people.

Perhaps in the end Tz'u Hsi wanted to be remembered as a sage Confucian ruler. If so, she had failed utterly to gauge the pulse of the times. She herself was the last real emperor of China; within three years, dynasty and state would collapse. For this Tz'u Hsi was heavily to blame. Although no one person can be held responsible for the mistakes made by China in the second half of the nineteenth century, Tz'u Hsi's blindness to the urgent needs of the country had unquestionably sealed the fate of the dynasty. She could have exercised her great influence in the cause of modernization; instead she had been interested only in her own power, profit, and pleasure. Had she allowed Kuang Hsü to rule, the Ch'ing might possibly have survived as a constitutional monarchy. Under a minor, the dynasty had no chance of dealing with the powerful tides of change that were sweeping China. The prophecy had been fulfilled: a woman of the clan of Yehe had brought about the fall of the Manchus. Their passing ushered in four decades of eclipse for Peking.

VI

End of the Imperial Era

Like the Mongols before them, the Manchus were overthrown from the south. In both cases it had taken a long time for the incoming dynasty to bring the south under firm control, and in both cases the southerners continued to regard themselves as the true guardians of the Chinese cultural heritage. K'ang-hsi and Ch'ien Lung had done a good job of convincing southerners that the Manchu rulers cherished that heritage as their own, but under the impact of imperialist aggression the carefully constructed Manchu-Chinese symbiosis began to come apart. During the Opium War, for example, it was the Chinese who were determined to resist foreign encroachment on their native soil — and the Manchus who were prepared to compromise with the imperialist powers because they feared a major conflict would weaken the dynasty.

Under the circumstances, it was hardly surprising that the Manchus clung to Confucian values, for Confucianism permitted people of any race to be part of Chinese civilization. If Confucianism were to be abandoned, then whatever replaced it would be a purely Chinese civilization in which the Manchus would no longer be legitimate members of the elite but merely foreign despots. Ironically enough, the south became dangerous to the Manchus precisely because the erosion of the Confucian system began in this stronghold of Chinese culture. The port of Canton was the Achilles' heel of the Manchu empire, pierced by Western ideas as well as Western weapons.

It was the citizens of South China who traveled abroad, and it was they who became the great business class of Southeast Asia. These overseas communities, patriotically Chinese but untraditional in outlook, pro-

vided much of the funding of the revolutionary activities that developed with the growth of the anti-Manchu movement in the latter half of the nineteenth century.

The man who eventually emerged as China's leading revolutionary was Sun Yat-sen. His background tailored him perfectly for this role. Sun was born in Kwangtung, near the foreign-held port of Macao, and he was brought up to revere the Taiping rebels, whose uprising began in Kwangtung. He was partly educated in a mission school in Honolulu, then studied medicine in Canton and Hong Kong, finally obtaining his degree from a mission hospital. Sun's travels and studies turned him into an anti-Manchu republican and a social revolutionary. His rallying cry was antiforeign nationalism — and the Manchus were included among the foreigners. The 1905 manifesto of Sun Yat-sen's revolutionary group, the T'ung-meng Hui, proclaimed the expulsion of the Manchus as its first objective.

The T'ung-meng Hui made a number of attempts to unseat the dynasty — all of them unsuccessful — and in the end the revolution started without Sun. On October 9, 1911, an anti-Manchu organization composed of Chinese troops stationed in Wuhan, an important industrial center on the Middle Yangtze, was accidentally uncovered, forcing the plotters' hand. They rose on October 10. Within five days, Wuhan was in their power. Their coup was quickly emulated in other important garrisons, and soon much of the southern half of the country had declared for a republic.

Yet the forces of the revolution were far from victory. Sun Yat-sen — who had been inaugurated as provisional president of the Chinese republic on January 1, 1912, after a hurried return from the United States

— appreciated the fact that the army in North China was still loyal to the dynasty, and he realized that in the event of civil war the outcome would be uncertain. The emperor's father, who ruled as regent in the Forbidden City, had proved incapable of firm action. Only one man seemed likely to end the stalemate: Yüan Shih-k'ai. Yüan had been in disgrace since the death of the empress dowager because of his betrayal of Kuang Hsü. Nevertheless, he still commanded strong support among the generals of the northern armies — which he had helped organize — and the regent turned to him as the only man with sufficient stature to save the dynasty. In mid-November Yüan became premier in Peking.

The revolutionaries, headquartered in Nanking, did not consider Yüan one of themselves, but they offered him the presidency of the republic if he could engineer the end of the dynasty. At first Yüan may have hoped to preserve a constitutional Ch'ing monarchy, but he soon realized that this would be impossible short of civil war — which he could lose. He therefore accepted the republican offer, thus betraying a second emperor.

The terms that Yüan won for the boy-emperor P'u-yi were generous. According to the Articles of Favorable Treatment there was to be no imperial bloodletting. The emperor was to retain his title and to receive a large annual subsidy. He would be permitted to reside for a time in the Forbidden City; later he would be obliged to move to the Summer Palace. The temples and mausoleums of the imperial family and the sacrificial rites appropriate to them would be maintained by the republic in perpetuity.

The imperial system disappeared with surprising ease. Whereas previous changes of dynasty had often involved decades of warfare, in the winter of 1911–12 some two thousand years of history were sloughed off in five months. On March 10, Yüan Shih-k'ai was sworn in as China's second president. Following the ceremony he reviewed a massive parade from the Gate of Heavenly Peace, the entrance to the Imperial City.

To many Chinese, the idea of a republic remained quite strange. An anecdote often told in Peking recalls that the workmen who were sent to the dynastic gate to replace the Ch'ing tablet with one for the republic felt uneasy about throwing the old one away. After all, what was this newfangled republic and how long would it last? The foreman ordered his men to store the tablet in the loft above the gate. There the workmen found another tablet, that of the Ming dynasty, which another cautious foreman had carefully put away almost three hundred years earlier. Both foremen were wise: the possibility of a Ming restoration had not been eliminated for several decades after the Manchu conquest, and there were two attempts at an imperial restoration after the 1911 revolution.

One major reason for Yüan Shih-k'ai's insistence upon such good abdication terms for the emperor was almost certainly because he did not want the imperial institution besmirched. He was probably already dreaming of ascending the dragon throne; his son hinted as much to foreign diplomats as early as mid-November 1911. In the first few months of 1913, Yüan attempted to hasten the departure of the emperor from the Forbidden City to the Summer Palace. As president, Yüan already occupied the palaces on the Chung Hai and Nan Hai, the Middle and South seas that lay

The harmonious balance between yin *and* yang —
*the two complementary forces that govern the
universe, according to ancient Chinese belief —
must have been seriously disrupted by the
dissolution of the monarchy in 1911. The
interlocking* yin-yang *symbols appear on the red
lacquer panel at right, surrounded by the* pa kua,
*the eight trigrams that hold the key to knowledge.
P'u-yi, the empress dowager's chosen successor,
became the pampered prisoner of the republic,
forbidden even to visit the Summer Palace (left).*

west of the Forbidden City. He may have thought that a move into the Forbidden City itself would have great symbolic significance, but he temporarily abandoned this aim at the insistence of one of his more powerful supporters, Chang Hsun, who was known as "the Pig-tailed General" because he had preserved his Manchu hairstyle out of loyalty to the dynasty.

Despite this setback, Yüan managed to consolidate his position considerably during the year. He had one prominent republican assassinated, and he easily suppressed the second revolution that erupted in a number of the southern provinces. As a result, Sun Yat-sen and his top advisers were forced to flee the country. Yüan then ordered Sun's Kuomintang party dissolved, and in January 1914 he suspended the national parliament. In September he stated that he intended to revive the state cult of Confucius, and two months later, in the manner of K'ang-hsi, he issued a set of moral instructions for the people. Finally, on December 12, 1915, Yüan accepted the "urging" of a national congress of representatives and agreed to revive the monarchy with himself as the first constitutional emperor of a new dynasty, the Hung-hsien.

Immensely costly preparations were made — including the redecoration of the three main halls on the Dragon Pavement — so that the emperor could start his reign in appropriate style. At dawn on December 23, Yüan got into an armored car and drove to the Temple of Heaven to perform the sacred rites of the winter solstice. Imperial yellow sand had been scattered over the route he traversed, and soldiers standing three-deep guarded every inch of the way in case any republican should decide to disrupt this ludicrous

charade. Dr. Jerome Ch'en, Yüan's biographer, continues the story:

At the southern gate of the temple, the president entered a vermilion coach, which carried him to the temple itself. Then he was carried into the building in a sedan chair and was helped up the marble steps by Generals Yin-ch'ang and Lu Chin. Once inside, he changed out of his field-marshal's uniform into the sacrificial robe and headgear. The robe was royal purple, adorned with 12 circular dragon designs, and the headgear was an oblong board on a tight-fitting cap, an ancient imperial design. The changes "appropriate to republicanism" amounted to the armored car, the purple color of the robe, the omission of the traditional nine strings of beads from the headgear, and the new wording of the prayers — "I, Yuan Shih-k'ai, representing the Republic of China," instead of "Your son and vassal."

Yüan's imperial dreams were swiftly and rudely shattered. He had ignored the opposition of the imperialist powers to the revival of the monarchy, but he could not ignore the military revolts that followed his ascent to the throne, for they achieved rapid successes. On March 22, 1916, Yüan decreed the end of the eighty-three-day-old Hung-hsien era. Within three months the Hung-hsien emperor was dead as well.

Monarchism was not quite finished, however. In June 1917, the Pig-tailed General, Chang Hsun, whose forces controlled much of East China, attempted to restore the Ch'ing dynasty. He ordered the president to dissolve parliament and he issued proclamations announcing that the boy-emperor had resumed the throne. Throughout Peking canny citizens put out

Although Yüan Shih-k'ai (far right), president of the republic, failed to reestablish a monarchy — with himself as emperor — a second attempt was launched soon after his death by Chang Hsun. A loyal supporter of the Ch'ing dynasty, the "Pig-tailed General" hoped to restore the boy-emperor P'u-yi (left) to the throne of his ancestors. But that endeavor collapsed when a rival general bombed the capital, causing damage to Chang Hsun's own palace (right).

dragon flags, improvised with paper and paste at the urging of the police; would-be courtiers rushed out to secondhand clothing shops to buy up Ch'ing court uniforms; and theatrical costumers were besieged by demands for false pigtails.

The restoration lasted only twelve days, and it was ended by the first aerial bombardment in Chinese military history. The most powerful general in North China, a man whom Chang Hsun had assumed was on his side, sent a single plane over Peking. It dropped three small bombs on the Forbidden City. According to P'u-yi, one of the bombs fell just outside the Gate of Honoring the Ancestors, not very far away from the boy-emperor's royal apartments in the Hall of the Cultivation of the Mind. That particular bomb wounded the carrier of a sedan chair; another damaged a pond in the Imperial Garden; the third fell on the roof of a gateway in the western section, terrifying a group of eunuchs who were gambling there. Fortunately for them, that bomb failed to explode. But the bombing mission did explode the restoration enterprise. Chang Hsun fled to the Dutch embassy, and although other generals encouraged the courtiers of the Forbidden City to preserve hopes of a restoration, they were always disappointed. The monarchy was gone for good.

For P'u-yi the restoration attempt of 1917 was a brief and exciting interlude in a dull and circumscribed adolescence. He occupied the palaces of his ancestors in the Forbidden City for thirteen years after the 1911 revolution, and he practically never ventured beyond its walls. He and his retainers were assigned the Inner Court in the northern part of the compound, for the southern ceremonial section with its three main halls

had been taken over by the republic and partially converted into a museum. P'u-yi's curious twilight existence during these years was later chronicled by Sir Reginald Johnston, who tutored the boy from 1919 until the latter's expulsion from the Forbidden City in November 1924.

P'u-yi's spartan diet of Chinese classical studies was broadened during his English lessons with Johnston, who used those periods to inform him about the outside world and, incidentally, to inspire him with a strong desire to emulate the manners and dress of an English gentleman. One concrete result of this infatuation with foreign fashions was that P'u-yi cut off his pigtail. Within a month, the 1,500 pigtails in the Forbidden City had been reduced to three, the holdouts being his sternly traditionalist teachers.

Johnston was very anxious that P'u-yi be moved to the Summer Palace, as agreed under the Articles of Favorable Treatment, for he felt that the environment there would be more advantageous to the boy-emperor's physical, mental, and moral welfare. The courtiers fought Johnston tooth and nail as they had fought Yüan Shih-k'ai, and for the same sort of reasons. Their conclusive argument was that the Summer Palace could not house the whole establishment of the Forbidden City — and they could not consider staff reductions. It was not until Johnston was appointed keeper of the Summer Palace in early 1924 that he was able to bludgeon the courtiers into allowing P'u-yi even to visit the place. During his years of imperial privilege, the walls of the Forbidden City had been more effective in keeping the emperor prisoner than they were in keeping his former subjects out — the visit to the

Summer Palace was P'u-yi's first trip outside Peking.

Under Johnston's tutelage, P'u-yi had become very dissatisfied with his confined existence and his corrupt entourage. In early 1923 he plotted to flee the Forbidden City and renounce his title, but he was frustrated by his courtiers, who knew that with the emperor gone their life of ease would end. In retaliation, P'u-yi decided to reform his establishment.

The court was run by the Imperial Household Department, whose top officials were Manchus. Most of the staff were Chinese eunuchs. Under the empress dowager, the power of the eunuchs at court had increased significantly, although it was never as great as it had been under the Ming. At the time of the revolution of 1911, there were three thousand eunuchs in the Forbidden City; after the founding of the republic their number was reduced to one thousand. The Imperial Household Department was notoriously corrupt, so much so that when one of the four surviving imperial consorts died in April 1921, looting eunuchs brawled with each other for the pick of their late mistress's treasures — in the very palace where her body was lying in state.

P'u-yi's attack on the Household Department started with an order to reduce the Forbidden City's enormous annual budget. Huge sums of money were spent on food, for example, great quantities of which went to waste. He also ordered a full inventory of the palace's treasures because he was well aware that many priceless pieces were finding their way to the Peking antique market. The items stored in the Palace of Established Happiness were to be catalogued first, but on the night of June 27, 1923, before the inventory could take place,

the palace went up in flames. Many other buildings were also burned, and but for the arrival of a fire engine from the Legation Quarter, the nearby palaces of the emperor and empress might have been destroyed as well.

It was estimated that well over six thousand items were lost, principally examples of Buddhist art, including nearly three thousand gold Buddhas or altar ornaments. P'u-yi snatched one benefit from the disaster: he had the burned-out area cleared and a tennis court built there, for he was most anxious to learn the game that Johnston had informed him was de rigueur for the English gentleman.

Furious that the Household Department had contrived to prevent discovery of its depredations, P'u-yi struck back. Within three weeks of the fire, on July 15, he acted in what would have been an historic manner had he been a reigning monarch: every eunuch on the household staff was paraded through one of the palace courtyards and informed that his services were no longer required. A body of friendly republican troops stood by to ensure there would be no protest, and within an hour the eunuchs had all left the Forbidden City. The eunuchs had not even been allowed to return to their rooms, for fear that they might use the opportunity for looting. For the next three or four days, they squatted on the parade ground between the north wall of the Forbidden City and Coal Hill, awaiting their turns to return briefly to the Forbidden City in small, carefully supervised groups to collect their personal belongings and any severance pay to which they might be entitled. P'u-yi made only one compromise: he permitted the three aging imperial consorts to re-

tain a few dozen eunuchs — without whom, they tearfully insisted, even the simplest actions of everyday life would be impossible.

However well-intentioned, P'u-yi remained an anachronism. Republican leaders came to feel that the emperor was an unnecessary carry-over from the past, and antimonarchist sentiment grew. The coup de grace was administered by "the Christian General," Fêng Yü-hsiang, who took over Peking on October 23, 1924. Fêng's troops first occupied Coal Hill, opposite the north wall of the Forbidden City. Within the palace the imperial court waited in trepidation, cutting short mourning ceremonies for a recently deceased imperial consort. Then, like Chang Hsun during the abortive 1917 restoration, Fêng dissolved parliament and forced the president to resign. On the morning of November 5, his troops disarmed the imperial guards at the gates of the Forbidden City. P'u-yi was shown a revision of the Articles of Favorable Treatment under which he had to agree to the abolition of his title. He was to leave the Forbidden City the same day, although he would continue to receive a subsidy from the state. P'u-yi signed, and at 3 P.M. he and the empress were driven out of the Forbidden City, past Coal Hill, and through the main north gate of the Imperial City. The central gateway — reserved exclusively for the emperor's use — was not opened for him, for he was now simply Mr. P'u-yi. The last emperor of China had finally left the imperial stage.

The ejection of the president and the dissolution of parliament were, in fact, more significant events in the history of the Chinese republic than the departure of P'u-yi from the Forbidden City. Because of them,

Peking lost its last shred of legitimacy as the capital of China, and the seat of government soon shifted elsewhere. From the beginning of the republic there had been many revolutionaries who wanted to change the capital. Liang Ch'i-chao, one of the intellectual leaders of the revolution, was one of them:

> The capital, Peking, has become the hotbed of all evils. Not only has the land lost its auspicious features and the water its sweet taste, but a thousand crimes, a myriad scandals, weird carbuncles and chronic diseases of this sinful world are also concentrated there. If the political centre stays there, China will never see a single day of clean government.

Men like Sun Yat-sen wanted a capital in the more revolutionary, anti-Manchu south, preferably in the key economic region of the Middle and Lower Yangtze. They favored Wuhan, where the revolution began, or Nanking, the first Ming capital. However, Yüan Shih-k'ai could not be budged from his power base in North China, and the imperialist powers were not anxious to vacate the comfortable Legation Quarter in Peking, so the capital stayed where it was. Eventually Peking itself became the country's most revolutionary city.

The warlord era, like the Warring States period over two thousand years earlier, was one of China's great periods of intellectual experimentation. In the sudden freedom produced by the removal of the age-old Confucian straitjacket, Chinese students and intellectuals ransacked the storehouses of foreign cultures to find new doctrines with which China might be saved. One of these students was a young southerner from Hunan province who started taking classes at Peking University in the autumn of 1918. To keep himself alive he

Dr. Sun Yat-sen, one of the earliest opponents of the Ch'ing dynasty and the spiritual leader of the Chinese Revolution, held elective office (as provisional president in 1912) in the new republic only briefly. Over the next decade he built his Nationalist party into a viable and effective political machine. Yet even he paid tribute to China's monarchal past by visiting the Ming Tombs at Nanking (left). Upon his death in 1925, his successor as Kuomintang head, Chiang Kai-shek, honored Dr. Sun's memory by constructing a massive mausoleum (right) in the style of the Ming Tombs.

took a job as an assistant in the university library. Years later, Mao Tse-tung recalled some of his impressions of the capital for an American journalist, the late Edgar Snow:

> My own living conditions in Peking were quite miserable, and in contrast the beauty of the old capital was a vivid and living compensation. I stayed in a place called "Three-Eye Well" (San Yen-ching), in a little room which held seven other people. When we were all packed fast on the k'ang [a raised platform of mud brick or clay heated from underneath] there was scarcely room enough for any of us to breathe. I used to have to warn people on each side of me when I wanted to turn over. But in the parks and the old palace grounds I saw the early northern spring, I saw the white plum blossoms flower while the ice still held solid over the North Sea (Pei Hai).

Among the intellectual leaders of Peking University who most impressed the twenty-five-year-old Mao were the head of the Department of Literature, Ch'ên Tu-hsiu, and Mao's own immediate superior, Li Ta-chao, the university librarian. The Bolshevik revolution had inspired both men to study Marxism, although neither was yet a Marxist. The event that propelled all three in the direction of communism occurred in Peking shortly after Mao had left for Shanghai and the south.

In late April 1919, news reached the capital that the Versailles Peace Conference had awarded the former German concessions in China to Japan. The Chinese, as cobelligerents against the Germans, had expected to have the territory restored. This affront to their national pride sparked a series of massive student demonstrations. On May 4 some three thousand students,

half the capital's student population, paraded in front of the Gate of Heavenly Peace and on through the Legation Quarter. They beat up pro-Japanese officials and clashed with the police, and soon similar protests erupted in other cities. Workers joined the students, and all classes of Chinese society collaborated in a student-led boycott of Japanese goods. This unprecedented demonstration of Chinese patriotism became known as the May Fourth Movement.

It was in this fever of anti-imperialism that many of China's intellectuals and students turned to Marxism. The Soviet Union encouraged them by declaring its intention of giving up all tsarist Russian concessions on Chinese soil. In July 1921, thirteen men assembled at a girls' school in the French concession in Shanghai for the first congress of the Chinese Communist party. At that time the newborn Communist party was almost three decades away from ultimate success. For the moment the hopes of most patriotic Chinese were centered on Sun Yat-sen and his Nationalist party, the Kuomintang. Since his break with Yüan Shih-k'ai, Sun's fortunes had undergone many vicissitudes. In the early twenties, he established himself in his native Kwangtung and set out to restructure the Nationalist party along Leninist lines. With Soviet advisers helping him, Sun also began to train a revolutionary army armed with Soviet weapons.

In 1925 Sun died, and conflicts between Nationalists and Communists soon began to emerge. Nevertheless, in July 1926 the Northern Expedition that Sun had dreamed of was launched under the leadership of his chief military colleague and brother-in-law, Chiang Kai-shek. By the end of 1928, the expedition had suc-

ceeded and China was nominally united from Manchuria to Canton.

Faithful to Sun's memory, Chiang Kai-shek established the republican capital at Nanking and built a mausoleum for Sun near the tomb of the Ming emperor who had first made Nanking an imperial capital. Peking, no longer the "Northern Capital," was once again called Peiping, or "Northern Peace," as it had been under Ming Hung Wu.

There was more than sentimentality behind Chiang's choice of Nanking. Chiang himself was from Chekiang province, and he drew much of his support from the Lower Yangtze region where Nanking was located. The Lower and Middle Yangtze was still the country's dominant economic area, and Nanking was close to China's most important opening to the West, the great port and industrial center of Shanghai. The choice of Nanking symbolized China's diminished interest in inner Asia, where Outer Mongolia and Tibet had thrown off Chinese rule, and its desire to modernize the Chinese heartland.

The move to Nanking was to some extent involuntary. Chiang's control of North and Northeast China was heavily dependent upon friendly warlords who might desert him at any time. Manchuria was increasingly dominated by Japanese and Soviet economic interests, and the Japanese had already indicated that they had even greater ambitions in the area. Peiping had once again become a frontier city.

From its inception, the Nanking government, like all its predecessors since 1839, was faced with the problem of coping simultaneously with internal unrest and external aggression. Chiang's policy was "unification

before resistance," and the main threat to unification was the Communists. In April 1927, he suddenly pounced on them, slaughtering hundreds in anti-Communist purges in Shanghai and elsewhere. Remnants of various Communist groups united under Mao Tsetung — by now an experienced promoter of peasant uprisings — in a mountain area in southern Kiangsi.

In October 1934, the Communist forces set out on one of the epics of revolutionary history, the Long March. Harried all the way by Chiang's soldiers, the Red army marched west to the borders of Tibet and then north, ending up one year and six thousand miles later in Shensi province. The Communists finally made their headquarters at Yenan, less than two hundred miles north of Sian, the site of ancient Ch'ang-an. They had started out 90,000 strong; when they reached Shensi there were only 20,000 of them left. But they had survived. And they still represented an obstacle to Chiang's quest for unification.

Before he could attempt the final destruction of the Communists, Chiang was compelled to reverse his priorities and put resistance before unification. Resistance in this case meant resistance to Japan, which had become a serious threat to China's territorial integrity. After the Russo-Japanese war of 1904–5, Japan had reached a secret agreement with Russia by which Manchuria would be divided into northern (Russian) and southern (Japanese) sections for the purposes of economic exploitation. In 1915, the Japanese had forced Yüan Shih-k'ai to accept most of their Twenty-one Demands, which strengthened their position in southern Manchuria. Then, as Chiang Kai-shek was completing his reunification of China in the late 1920's, the Japa-

nese began to tighten their hold over Manchuria.

In June 1928, the commander of the Japanese forces protecting Japan's interests in Manchuria organized the assassination of Chang Tso-lin, the local warlord. Chang's son, "the Young Marshal" Chang Hsueh-liang, responded by declaring his adherence to the new Nationalist government of China. In the wake of the Young Marshal's declaration, the Japanese army decided that it had to take further action if its position were not to be eroded by growing Chinese nationalism.

On September 18, 1931, the army contrived for a bomb to explode on a portion of the track of the Japanese-owned Manchurian railway. The Chinese were blamed and the local Japanese commander used this as a pretext to take over all of Manchuria, despite opposition from the government in Tokyo. P'u-yi, who had been living in the Japanese concession in Tientsin, was persuaded to go north to Manchuria, there to become, first, the chief executive, and then, in 1934, emperor of the new state of Manchukuo. He "reigned" until 1945, when he was taken prisoner by the Russians, who eventually handed him over to the Chinese Communists.

After the Young Marshal and his troops were expelled from Manchuria by the Japanese, Chiang Kai-shek tried to use them to fight the Communists in North China. But in December 1936, when Chiang came to Chang Hsueh-liang's headquarters in Sian, the Young Marshal took him prisoner in an attempt to pressure him into agreeing to a united front with the Communists against the Japanese. Chiang would sign nothing, and he eventually persuaded the Young Marshal to release him. But the tide of public opinion was so strongly in favor of national resistance to Japan that a united front between the Nationalists and the Communists was finally negotiated.

On July 7, 1937, an incident occurred at the Marco Polo Bridge outside Peiping. Chinese soldiers and the Japanese troops who were stationed at the bridge under the terms of the Boxer Protocol fired upon one another, and the Japanese took this as justification for invading North China. Peiping fell easily into their hands, and before the end of the year it had become the seat of a puppet government. It remained under Japanese occupation until 1945.

Chiang Kai-shek's wartime strategy was "to sell space to buy time." After putting up brave resistance in the early years of the war, he retreated up the Yangtze and established his capital at Chungking in the Szechwan rice bowl. There he waited for what he was convinced would be the inevitable defeat of Japan in the world war he was certain must come. As a result of his policy of masterly inactivity, much of the credit for fighting the Japanese went to the Communists, whose popularity increased substantially. The uneasy united front was soon marred by clashes between Mao's forces and Chiang's, and both sides began preparing for the postwar struggle. After Japan's defeat, Mao and Chiang met briefly in Chungking. For a time the Americans tried to mediate, but the two leaders knew that they would never collaborate again.

Strategically Chiang's greatest mistake turned out to be the reoccupation of the cities of the north and northeast. He managed to garrison them, but the Communists quickly took control of the surrounding countryside, isolating the garrisons from one another. By late 1948 all Manchuria had fallen to the forces of Lin Piao, the Communists' most brilliant general. Lin's army now closed in on Peiping. The defenders mounted artillery on the city walls, and on December 13 the siege began. Lin Piao was determined to avoid destroying the architectural treasures of the Forbidden City, and the city's defenders knew it. A Chinese observer commented that the garrison commander "holds a beautifully delicate and priceless vase in his fingers. If anyone tries to take it, it will be destroyed."

The siege lasted for six weeks. The Communist forces never used their artillery; instead they kept trying to get the garrison commander to surrender. The commander reportedly changed his mind nine times. At one stage, when it seemed that the garrison commander was determined to resist to the last man, Lin Piao became impatient and began drawing up plans for breaching the city walls. He consulted one of China's leading architects to discover whether the place picked for the assault should be avoided for cultural reasons. The architect criticized the chosen site on the grounds that it was one of the few surviving pieces of unrestored Ming architecture, and Lin accepted an alternative location. Fortunately, the surrender of the city on January 22 made an assault unnecessary.

Eight months later, on October 1, 1949, Mao Tsetung stood on the terrace of the Gate of Heavenly Peace and proclaimed the birth of the People's Republic of China. Peiping became Peking, the capital of the country once again. Like Ming loyalists three hundred years earlier, the Nationalists sought refuge on the island of Taiwan, taking with them many of the treasures of the Forbidden City.

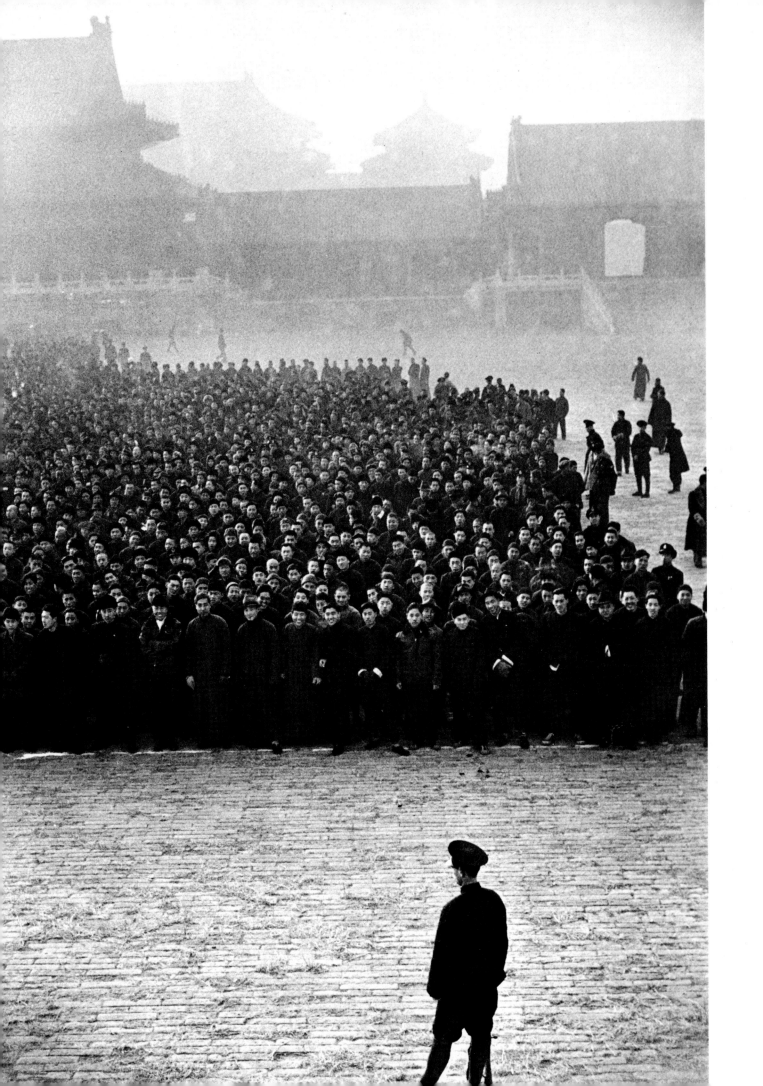

VII

The Unforbidden City

The Communist victory had something of the flavor of the founding of a dynasty. The Chinese Revolution had not been manufactured, Soviet-style, among the workers of the big cities; it had been achieved with peasant armies. When Mao threw away the Soviet rule book, he found inspiration in traditional Chinese sagas and historical records. He armed the peasants and established a power base, using tactics that owed more to Sun Tzu, a Chinese strategist of the fourth century B.C., than to Clausewitz. He won over large sections of the educated elite and, finally, defeated the government of the day in pitched battle.

For the Chinese people there was a familiar ring to the Communist movement. It had a revered leader, as the empire had; it was guided by a body of doctrine that claimed universal relevance, in the manner of Confucianism; and it relied upon an elite whose claim to rule, like that of the mandarins, was founded on their knowledge of that doctrine. But the novel elements in the Communist revolution were more important than the traditional ones. Confucians had looked back nostalgically to a golden age they could never restore; the Communists looked forward to a glorious future they were determined to build. Confucianism was the ideology of an agrarian society that feared social change; communism stressed industrialization and prescribed overturning ancient traditions and customs in order to build a new society.

Mao's strength was his ability to fuse Marxism-Leninism with Chinese reality. Steeped in Chinese history, he was able to strike the right chords in the Chinese people. Adept in Leninism, he organized the best-disciplined proletarian vanguard in the world to guide the Chinese people where he wanted them to go. The Confucian bureaucracy had exercised only shadowy control at the grass roots level; the Communists had cells in almost every village in China. Within a very short time after the revolution, the Communist government was established more firmly than any dynasty had ever been.

For the first time Peking was the ideal capital for a native Chinese regime. Manchuria had been Sinicized by almost a hundred years of Chinese immigration, which had submerged the Manchus almost without a trace, and it had been industrialized during two decades of Japanese colonialism. In terms of industrial power and agricultural surplus, the northeast and the Yangtze provinces were like the two ends of a dumbbell — with Peking at the point of grip.

The new regime had other reasons for the inner-Asian orientation which the choice of Peking implied. For one thing, Sinkiang and the northeast were firmly in the government's grasp; Tibet, it confidently and correctly expected, soon would be. True, Outer Mongolia had broken away, but in the flush of victory China's leaders probably hoped that it would eventually be reunited with China. More importantly, the non-Chinese territories beyond the Great Wall were no longer a menace. With the firm extension of Russian and Chinese control into central and eastern Asia, the great nomad melting pot had dried up. In the twentieth century the North China plain was at last safe from barbarian horsemen, and the Soviet Union, the power that had replaced the nomads across the wall, was to be the new China's closest ally, providing the aid that China had previously sought from the West.

Political common sense also dictated the choice of Peking, for the Communists' strength lay in North China. Mao and a large number of his top colleagues were southerners, but for the previous fourteen years they had operated in North China, gradually extending their control until as early as 1945 they governed almost 100,000,000 people. By contrast, the Communists knew that it would be some time before they ferreted out all of Chiang Kai-shek's supporters in the former Nationalist strongholds of central China. Moreover, Nanking had been the capital of an enemy regime whose memory had to be erased by its conquerors. Indeed, the Communists must have felt about Nanking much as Sun Yat-sen felt about Peking — namely that the stink of corruption still about it might be contaminating.

Mao also felt drawn to Peking because of its distinguished history. For all his opposition to the imperial system Mao retained a deep respect for China's past, and however strong the economic pull of the Yangtze region, North China was the cradle of Chinese civilization. Mao's pride in Chinese history doubtless does much to account for the care and money that the Communists lavished on the restoration of the Forbidden City and other great monuments in Peking after the ravages of the warlord era. Every effort was made to reproduce the architectural effects of imperial times, but some proved too elusive. A respected observer regretted that it had not been possible to recreate the old colors; where roofs had to be repaired, for example, the glorious imperial gold had been replaced with a dull pinkish yellow, and the repainted walls were a lifeless brown red instead of the rose red of the imperial era.

Today the term Forbidden City is a misnomer, for virtually the entire complex is open to the public as the Palace Museum. The most northerly of the three halls on the Dragon Pavement houses a museum of ancient arts and crafts, and other former imperial or sacred precincts have been similarly transformed. Just south of the Forbidden City, on the east side of the main axis, stands the former Imperial Ancestral Temple, now known as the People's Palace of Culture. It houses not dynastic tablets but theaters, sports arenas, and other recreational facilities. On the opposite side of the main axis, the Altar of Earth and Grain remains as a park named in honor of Sun Yat-sen. The park around Coal Hill has special amusements for children; the Pei Hai is a popular lake for rowing excursions. The architectural magnificence of the Temple of Heaven was also fully restored, although it is thought to have been damaged during the Great Proletarian Cultural Revolution of 1966–69. The white marble terrace surrounding its magnificent, triple-roofed Hall of Prayer for Good Harvests has been used as a dance floor in the summertime.

Throngs of Chinese sightseers have given a new and different kind of life to the old strongholds of imperial majesty. But if power has disappeared from the Forbidden City, it has not gone far. Mao Tse-tung and his senior colleagues live within the confines of the old Imperial City, along the shores of the Chung Hai and the Nan Hai. But only a privileged few among the hundreds of foreign visitors they meet every year call on them there. Mao Tse-tung's late biographer, the American journalist Edgar Snow, has described Mao's residence as "a graceful old one-story yellow-roofed

The enlarged quadrangle of the T'ien An Men
(below), at the southern entrance to the Imperial
City, is Peking's equivalent of Red Square in
Moscow. On October 1 of each year, the citizenry
gather there en masse to commemorate the 1949
founding of the People's Republic of China.

The rise of Mao Tse-tung (left) from obscure peasant origins to the leadership of 800,000,000 Chinese has won him more adulation than that accorded all the Sons of Heaven combined. In the process of transforming a backward nation into an industrial power, his regime has altered the look of the capital as well. Among the many additions to the no-longer-forbidden Forbidden City is the Monument to the People's Heroes (right), a 120-foot marble monolith south of the T'ien An Men.

residence . . . one of a group of palace buildings formerly occupied by court mandarins and later by Kuomintang officials." According to Snow, "The large, comfortable living room of Mao's home is tastefully furnished in Chinese style; directly adjoining it are a small dining room and his study and living quarters. The meals he eats and serves his guests are a few home-style dishes of Hunanese cooking."

Snow had earlier rejected Nationalist charges that Mao's style of living justified the adjective "lavish." As he pointed out, if Mao had wanted to he could have used the palaces of the Forbidden City. Mao's home on the Nan Hai is within walking distance of T'ien An Men Square, where Communist leaders review and receive the masses. Here, not far south of the great throne room of the Hall of Supreme Harmony, is Mao's "audience chamber." Appropriately, T'ien An Men, the Gate of Heavenly Peace and the ancient southern gateway to the Imperial City, occupies the central position in the national emblem of the People's Republic. On the T'ien An Men hang a large portrait of Mao and two banners proclaiming: "Long Live the People's Republic of China" and "Long Live the Great Unity of the Peoples of the World." Above, on the terrace, Mao and his colleagues view the marchers who pass along Ch'ang-an Street on state occasions.

In front of the T'ien An Men is a vast square, enlarged by the Communists from twenty-seven acres to one hundred and paved with marked stones that indicate where demonstrators should position themselves. On the south side of the square is the 120-foot Monument to the People's Heroes, built to last as long as the Ming Tombs.

In 1959, two enormous buildings were added on the east and west sides of T'ien An Men Square in time for the regime's tenth anniversary celebration. To the east is a structure housing museums of Chinese history and the Chinese Revolution; to the west is the Great Hall of the People. The Great Hall, meeting place of the national legislature, took less than a year to design and build, but it has more floor space than all the palaces of the Forbidden City put together.

Peking has recovered its former position at the center of the Chinese polity, but it is a very different city from what it was. As capital of a new regime bent upon changing the face of China politically, economically, and socially, Peking could hardly have remained merely a beautifully restored imperial city. Since 1949 the boundaries of the Peking administrative area have been gradually enlarged until they now embrace some 9,500 square miles and 7,000,000 people. There has been building and rebuilding within the old city, but by far the most spectacular growth has been outside the walls. According to one former Western resident, by the mid-1950's Peking had undergone "a transformation such as Napoleon accomplished when he turned the walls of Paris into boulevards and laid out the wide and spacious avenues of the modern city." The comparison has become even more apt, for recently the wall between the inner and outer cities has been pulled down to permit construction of an underground railway. Sadly, the outer walls of Peking, which Lin Piao strove so hard to protect, are also coming down in the interests of better communications with the new suburban sections of the capital that have grown up in the past twenty-three years.

To the west there has been a tremendous expansion of educational and technical facilities. Many of the country's most prominent facilities of higher learning, research laboratories, and institutes are in this area. Peking has long been the country's leading intellectual center; recent developments have only served to accentuate that fact.

It is, however, the growth to the east that has changed Peking's character, making it into a great and highly modern industrial city. No longer is the capital a parasite, feeding on the economic surplus of other parts of the country as it did for five hundred years. Instead, it is one of the country's most productive areas. Before 1949, it was known for such handicraft products as enamel and lacquerware. Industry was limited to minor consumer goods. Now Peking produces iron and steel, cotton textiles, and various kinds of machinery. Pollution of the air over the capital has been minimized by concentrating industry east of the metropolitan area — so that the prevailing west winds blow smoke and fumes away from the city.

Politically, Peking has been a natural pacemaker for the nation. P'eng Chen, the city's mayor and party boss for the sixteen years directly preceding the start of the Great Cultural Revolution in mid-1966, spearheaded the great campaigns of mass mobilization that the Communists conducted during his tenure. One of his finest hours came in early 1956, when he hustled Peking businessmen into partnership with the state in two weeks — after the planners had said it would take two years to effect such a change.

P'eng Chen acquired his organizational techniques the hard way, mobilizing workers and students in Na-tionalist territory — and spending some years in Nationalist jails as a result. After 1949 he rose rapidly within the national party's politburo. As mayor of Peking, P'eng played host to countless foreign dignitaries, and his grinning features were probably seen more often in the party press than those of any other leader except Premier Chou En-lai.

P'eng seems to have taken a tough, down-to-earth stance on most issues. In early 1957, Mao wanted to rectify the faults of the Communist bureaucracy. He called upon non-Communists to voice criticisms, encouraging them with the slogan "Let a hundred flowers bloom, let a hundred schools contend." Mao believed that the Hungarian revolt underlined the need for all Communists to reform abuses; P'eng disagreed. Just back from a tour of Eastern Europe, he argued that soliciting criticism could be dangerous. Mao prevailed, and for a time intellectuals spoke out all over China. Students at Peking University posted their opinions on a "democratic wall" and listened to the more outspoken critics at an open-air forum. Some of these students apparently felt that they were continuing the revolutionary traditions of the May Fourth Movement, and there was talk of demonstrating in the streets when the national legislature met. Mao, seeing that the criticism was getting out of hand, agreed to halt the movement, but he rejected P'eng Chen's demand for severe treatment of all critics.

Despite their disagreements over the "Hundred Flowers," P'eng Chen appears to have supported Mao in 1958 when he launched the Great Leap Forward, an attempt to achieve an economic breakthrough by mass mobilization of labor. The inhabitants of Peking, like

people throughout China, set up crude blast furnaces — often quite literally in their own backyards — in an attempt to boost China's steel production. Later Peking and other cities experimented with urban communes in imitation of the rural communes that organized peasant efforts during the Great Leap Forward. These urban communes set up communal mess halls, nurseries, old people's homes, and various community services designed to free women from household tasks so that they might take part in the nationwide effort to boost all types of production.

The Great Leap Forward did help to boost production, but it also caused serious economic problems. These were gravely aggravated during the Three Bitter Years (1959–61) by some of the worst natural disasters in living memory. Mao was able to fend off the wide-ranging attack made by Defense Minister P'êng Têh-huai in 1959, and he immediately replaced P'êng with his long-time friend and colleague, Lin Piao. But as the economic situation worsened, an increasing number of party officials came to feel that P'êng Têh-huai had been justified. In the early 1960's, three officials in the Peking administration began to criticize Mao in veiled terms, publishing articles in the local press under the general title "Three Family Village" and using a common pseudonymous byline. One notorious article was entitled "Great Empty Talk" and contained a poem ridiculing Mao Tse-tung's famous foreign policy slogan, "The east wind prevails over the west wind."

Mao has been an avid newspaper reader all his life, so one assumes that he was aware of some of these attacks at the time they occurred. What is certain is that in the early 1960's he became progressively more concerned about the decline of revolutionary morale, especially among party officials, in the aftermath of the Great Leap Forward. He became obsessed with the notion that there was some danger of a "capitalist restoration" in China, something that he believed was already taking place in the Soviet Union. He attributed Soviet "revisionism" to degenerate leadership and a bureaucratic party machine, and he took measures to prevent the Soviet today from becoming the Chinese tomorrow.

The most important task was to make certain that the next generation of leaders would be truly revolutionary successors. Mao launched a socialist education campaign and demanded that writers and artists produce works that would truly inspire the people. P'eng Chen, despite somewhat dubious qualifications for the job, was ordered to direct the revision of the Peking Opera's repertoire.

By mid-1965, Mao seems to have despaired of revitalizing the country with the nation's leadership and the Communist party in their existing condition. Purging both would be difficult, however, since he had earlier allowed his potential victims to take control of the party machine. P'eng Chen in particular kept a very tight grip on the Peking party, which was later described by critics as an "independent kingdom" through which "no needle could pierce and no drop of water could trickle."

Mao was therefore forced to launch his attack from outside Peking and in stages. First, a playwright who had obliquely criticized the dismissal of P'eng Têh-huai was denounced in an article in a Shanghai paper in November 1965. Peking officials desperately tried to

find out who had put the Shanghai party up to allowing this, but even as they did so the attack broadened to include other authors of the "Three Family Village." Finally, P'eng Chen came under fire for defending his subordinates and was dramatically dismissed in May 1966. Six months later P'eng and several other senior officials were held up to public obloquy at a mass rally in a Peking stadium.

After the fall of P'eng Chen, Peking witnessed some of the most extraordinary scenes in its eventful history. At a series of huge rallies in T'ien An Men Square, often attended by a million people, Mao inspected the newly organized student shock troops of the Great Proletarian Cultural Revolution — the Red Guards — and revealed that he had picked a new successor, Lin Piao. The Red Guards hailed Mao with delirious shouts of *Mao Chu-hsi wan sui"* — "Ten thousand years to Chairman Mao" — and called him their "Great Teacher, Great Leader, Great Supreme Commander, Great Helmsman." They naturally did not call him by the ancient circumlocution for the emperor — Lord of Ten Thousand Years — but they did give Mao greater public adulation than any Chinese emperor had ever dreamed of. After the Cultural Revolution was over, Mao would tell Edgar Snow that his personality cult had been a necessary weapon against the party bureaucracy; it was a nuisance, but it was hard for people to overcome the habits of three thousand years of emperor-worshiping tradition. One day he hoped he would be known only as teacher.

Shortly after the first rally in T'ien An Men Square in August 1966, the Red Guards went into action in Peking — "learning revolution by making revolution."

Brandishing as their talisman the little red book of Mao's quotations, they covered the walls of the city with big-character posters presenting the residents of the capital with an ultimatum: all remnants of bourgeois society must be destroyed within a week. Shopkeepers were ordered to stop selling cosmetics and "outlandish" Western fashions, restaurants were ordered to simplify menus, signs were ripped down from shopfronts, and "odious imperialist street names" were changed. (The Street of the Prince's Well became Prevent Revisionism Street, for example.) The Red Guards began defacing Peking's remaining churches, mosques, Buddhist temples, and private homes — and they reportedly went to work on the Forbidden City for a brief period before being ejected. The Palace Museum became a forbidden city again for the duration of the Cultural Revolution.

Red Guards flooded into Peking from all over the country to derive inspiration from Mao and instruction from the Peking trailblazers. Soon they too were invading their local party headquarters and dragging out offending officials, whom they paraded through the streets in that traditional symbol of humiliation, the dunce's cap.

Peking was once again the storm center of revolution, seeming in those heady days to recapture some of the atmosphere of the May Fourth Movement — the main protagonists were, after all, revolutionary students — but also a little of the Boxers' urgent desire to purify the country. Some officials may have perished, but much of the loss of life during the Cultural Revolution seems to have been caused by internecine warfare between rival Red Guard factions. Mao eventually

had to call in the army to restore order, but by then the party had been thoroughly purged and the chairman could start trying to build a more egalitarian, less hierarchical society.

The Red Guards resembled the Boxers in other ways, notably in their antiforeign activities. Many embassies and their staffs suffered at their hands, although no one was killed. The worst incident occurred when extremists in the Foreign Ministry incited Red Guards to burn the British mission and attack some of its diplomats. This time there was no multinational relief column marching up from Tientsin, and only the Soviet Union was in a position to retaliate.

Sino-Soviet relations had gone from bad to worse since 1960, as the Chinese denounced Soviet willingness to compromise the vital interests of the Communist bloc in their dealings with America. Verbal polemics had been succeeded by minor border incidents, and early in the Cultural Revolution the Soviet delegates found that the road in front of their embassy had been renamed Struggle Against Revisionism Street. Red Guards held a massive demonstration there, carrying portraits of Stalin and Mao and shouting anti-Soviet slogans. Tension between the two countries increased until 1969, when it spilled over into major border clashes with serious loss of life.

At that time Soviet diplomats reportedly sounded out their Eastern European allies on their attitude toward some form of preemptive action against China. The obvious target seemed to be China's nuclear installations in the northwest, not too far from the territories of the Soviet Union and its ally Mongolia. A respected Japanese China-watcher, possibly recalling the ease with which Japan had penetrated North China in the 1930's, suggested that the Russians might even strike for the capital, with the intention of setting up a puppet regime. Peking, which had looked like such a well-placed capital in 1949, suddenly seemed as exposed to the Russians as Chung-tu had been to Genghis Khan or Ming Peking had been to the Manchus. Malign influences from the north momentarily threatened the Forbidden City once again—but this time saner councils prevailed, and the anticipated attack never came.

It was partly concern that the Soviet menace had merely been averted, not terminated, that led China to respond to cautious American overtures in 1971. In mid-July of that year it was revealed that Henry Kissinger, foreign affairs adviser to President Nixon, had secretly flown to Peking from Pakistan. As a result of his trip, the President himself would visit China within nine months and the United States would cease to oppose China's membership in the United Nations. It was a stunning international triumph for Mao, for despite the superior wealth and power of the United States the American President was to come to Peking—and clearly at the Chinese leader's suggestion.

When the visit did take place in the last week of February 1972, it marked, above all, the end of 130 years of humiliation and boycott. China, now armed with nuclear weapons and missiles and able to send satellites into space, had entered the comity of nations, certain of the respect that her stature justified. It meant, of course, that China would be accepting other countries as equals, which the rulers in the Forbidden City had held out against. But perhaps Mao Tse-tung, the self-styled "lone monk walking the world with a leaky um-

brella," was inwardly confident that one day his teachings would provide the world with the basis for a new universal civilization in which the old capital of the Middle Kingdom would once again be a fount of wisdom.

To achieve that destiny the Middle Kingdom would first have to survive the death, in 1976, of Chairman Mao. The question, long pondered by Chinese and China-watchers alike, of what would become of the ship of state in the absence of the Great Helmsman was not to receive a satisfactory answer until the end of the decade. With the resignation of Mao's hand-picked successor in September 1980, power in the Politburo seemed concentrated in the hands of Teng Hsiao-ping and his appointees. Teng, who had labored as Vice Premier to de-emphasize Maoist ideology, appeared determined to put China on course toward modernization.

Ross Terrill, a noted Sinologist and biographer of Mao who identifies several "Asias"—British Asia, French Asia, and, since World War II, American Asia—recently asserted that Peking remains outside the West's "tamed" Asia:

> It looks up to nobody, rests content with its own values and culture. Not foreign products, but Chinese, fill the fast-selling spots in the department stores. . . .
>
> In the present era of the West's decline in Asia, China emerges carrying the torch of Asia's confidence in itself. Peking, which was never really part of the "Asias," turns out to be the heart of Asia.

And the Forbidden City remains the heart of Peking.

THE FORBIDDEN CITY
IN LITERATURE

Adolescent visions of exotic adventures in distant lands rarely materialize. But for Marco Polo, the seventeen-year-old scion of wealthy Venetian merchants, the dream came true. With his uncle and father, the young man set out for China in 1271, arriving four years later at the brilliant court of Kublai Khan. Marco spent seventeen years in the service of the Mongol emperor, and was sent on various diplomatic missions throughout the empire. Insisting that "I have not told the half of what I saw," Marco later recorded his impressions, including a description of the emperor's palace at Ta-tu, the precursor of Peking's Forbidden City.

You must know that for three months of the year, to wit December, January, and February, the Great Kaan resides in the capital city of Cathay, which is called CAMBALUC [Ta-tu], and which is at the north-eastern extremity of the country. In that city stands his great Palace, and now I will tell you what it is like.

It is enclosed all round by a great wall forming a square, each side of which is a mile in length; that is to say, the whole compass thereof is four miles. . . .

You must know that it is the greatest Palace that ever was. Towards the north it is in contact with the outer wall, whilst towards the south there is a vacant space which the Barons and the soldiers are constantly traversing. The Palace itself hath no upper story, but is all on the ground floor, only the basement is raised some ten palms above the surrounding soil and this elevation is retained by a wall of marble raised to the level of the pavement, two paces in width and projecting beyond the base of the Palace so as to form a kind of terrace-walk, by which people can pass round the building, and which is exposed to view, whilst on the outer edge of the wall there is a very fine pillared balustrade; and up to this the people are allowed to come. The roof is very lofty, and the walls of the Palace are all covered with gold and silver. They are also adorned with representations of dragons sculptured and gilt, beasts and birds, knights and idols, and sundry other subjects. And on the ceiling too you see nothing but gold and silver and painting. On each of the four sides there is a great marble staircase leading to the top of the marble wall, and forming the approach to the Palace.

The Hall of the Palace is so large that it could easily dine 6000 people; and it is quite a marvel to see how many rooms there are besides. The building is altogether so vast, so rich, and so beautiful, that no man on earth could design anything superior to it. The outside of the roof also is all coloured with vermilion and yellow and green and blue and other hues, which are fixed with a varnish so fine and exquisite that they shine like crystal, and lend a resplendent lustre to the Palace as seen for a great way round. This roof is made too with such strength and solidity that it is fit to last forever.

On the interior side of the Palace are large buildings with halls and chambers, where the Emperor's private property is placed, such as his treasures of gold, silver, gems, pearls, and gold plate, and in which reside the ladies and concubines. There he occupies himself at his own convenience, and no one else has access.

Between the two walls of the enclosure which I have described, there are fine parks and beautiful trees bearing a variety of fruits. There are beasts also of sundry kinds, such as white stags and fallow deer. . . .

MARCO POLO
The Book of Ser Marco Polo, 1296–99

Calligraphic details and imperial scenes from a Manchu scroll illustrate pages 138–59; the sample of calligraphy that appears on page 160 is from a T'ang scroll.

138

Half a century after Marco Polo had returned to Venice, a native dynasty known as the Ming ousted the alien Mongols from China, renamed the capital Peking, and built the Forbidden City on the grounds of Kublai Khan's fabled palaces. The first European to enter that restricted domain was the Jesuit missionary Matthew Ricci. In 1601, eighteen years after his arrival in China, he was granted permission to build a mission house and church in the capital. His scientific knowledge of mathematics and astronomy and his scholarly reputation — he was one of the first Westerners to fully master written and spoken Chinese — earned him the grudging respect of the Son of Heaven and his subjects.

The royal palace in Pekin is entirely surrounded by four walls. During the daytime any man is permitted to pass beyond the first two walls, excepting the sacrificers to idols, who shave their heads. Women are excluded at all times. Only the palace eunuchs are allowed to go in beyond the first two walls. At night only soldiers and eunuchs are permitted to remain within the outer walls. The Fathers [Ricci and another priest named Pantoja] were permitted to pass beyond the second outer wall but no further. Here in one of the courtyards they met a multitude of people who had gathered to see the clocks [brought by Ricci as gifts for the emperor], and here the King sent one of his high-ranking eunuchs to receive them, one of those who kept him constant company and for whose prudence he had high regard. His name was Licin, and he received them most graciously in the name of the King. He wanted to know what their purpose was in bringing presents to the King, and they told him they were foreigners from the Great Occident, as the Chinese call Europe, that they were God-fearing men who adored the Director of heaven and earth, with no interest in worldly goods, and neither asking nor expecting presents in return, nor awaiting any recompense. He was quite pleased with this answer and gladly accepted the presents. They told him that the clocks were the invention of very clever artisans, for indicating the time, by day and by night, without anyone's assistance, and that they sounded the hours of themselves on bells, and pointed out the divisions of the hours with an indicator. They explained also that these machines had to be regulated by some one, that this was not a difficult operation, and that the servants could readily learn it in two or three days. All this was reported to His Majesty, who appointed four eunuchs from the College of Mathematicians of the palace, with orders to bring these instruments to his reception room, in three days, and to pay strict attention to the duty assigned them. . . .

During the three days of the lessons and for some days following, the King sent messengers to the Fathers inquiring about everything that happened to come into his head relative to Europe; the customs, the fertility of the land, architecture, clothes, precious stones, marriage and funerals, and European kings. The eunuchs asked all sorts of questions about the Fathers themselves, and those who were employed in their living quarters kept the sovereign informed of the most insignificant and ridiculous things that were happening, even to reporting how often they ate and drank and how much food they consumed. It was the curious, reporting to one more curious than themselves. The Fathers asked the eunuchs if they would inform the King that their own great desire was to live and die in Pekin, and that they wanted nothing else of him. . . .

The three days assigned for instructions had not passed before the King called for the clocks. They were brought to him at his order and he was so pleased with them that he immediately promoted the eunuchs and raised their wages. This they were delighted to report to the Fathers. . . . [who] became very important figures in the royal palace.

His Majesty was so taken by the novelty of the clocks that he wanted to see, not only the other presents but also the strangers who had brought them. His curiosity was by no means sated by what the eunuchs had told him. Yet he refused to break a custom which he had instituted several years before, namely, of never appearing in the company of anyone, save in that of the eunuchs and the concubines. Moreover, he did not wish to favor foreigners over his Magistrates, and so he put aside his wish and continued his persistent solitude. Instead of calling the Fathers, he sent two of the best artists he had, to paint full length pictures of both of them, in full detail, and then to bring the pictures to him. The Chinese are not adept at portrait painting, but in this instance they produced fairly good results. At first sight of the pictures, the King said, "Hoei, hoei. [Yes, yes.] It is quite evident that they are Saracens." The foreigners who came into China from Persia . . . bear a much closer resemblance to Europeans than they do to the Chinese, because of their facial contour and also because of their heavy beards. The eunuch, who was standing beside the King, told him that they were not Saracens, because they ate pork. He then wanted to know how the kings in Europe dressed and whether or not the Fathers had brought along any models of royal palaces. The first question was difficult to answer by description, but one of the Mission servants remembered that they had a picture, dedicated to the Holy Name, which showed angels and men and souls in purgatory, calling upon the Holy Name, and in which were represented European kings and also the Pope and a Duke and an Emperor, with their faces and vestments clearly depicted. This also gave the Fathers an opportunity to explain who He was, whose name was being venerated by the Christian princes, that is, the one who governed heaven and earth and the nether regions as well, and whose name the King of China himself should not hesitate to honor.

Father Matthew wrote out a brief explanation of all this, which was sent with the picture to the King, but he could not appreciate the fine traits of a small figure nor the variation in shading, which the Chinese ignore, so he ordered his royal artists to paint a copy of it, larger and with more coloring. They set to work on this immediately and the Fathers were detained in the palace for three days, supervising their efforts. In this way they showed the King and explained to him what the Fathers could not make him understand. They also supplied him with the information he desired relative to the palaces in Europe. Fortunately, they happened to have a picture of a palace in Spain [El Escorial], named after Saint Lawrence, an elegant print, representing several views, but they found out afterwards that the eunuch kept this for himself, because he could not explain it to his Master. He did, however, present the sovereign with a picture of the Church of Saint Mark and the square in Venice, together with some standards of the Venetian Republic. They say the King laughed when he heard that the princes of Europe lived on upper floors. He thought that going up and down stairs was quite inconvenient, if not dangerous. It is strange how people hold to the customs that please them.

MATTHEW RICCI
Journals, 1583–1610

唐明皇楊貴妃天寶九年忤旨送歸外第溫吉與中貴
人善溫入奏曰婦人智識不遠有忤聖情然貴妃久承
恩顧何惜宮中一席之地上即令中使張韜光賜御
饌妃附韜光泣奏曰妾忤聖顏罪當萬死衣服之外
皆聖恩所賜惟髮膚父母所育乃引刀剪髮一繚附獻
明皇見之驚惋即使力士召還

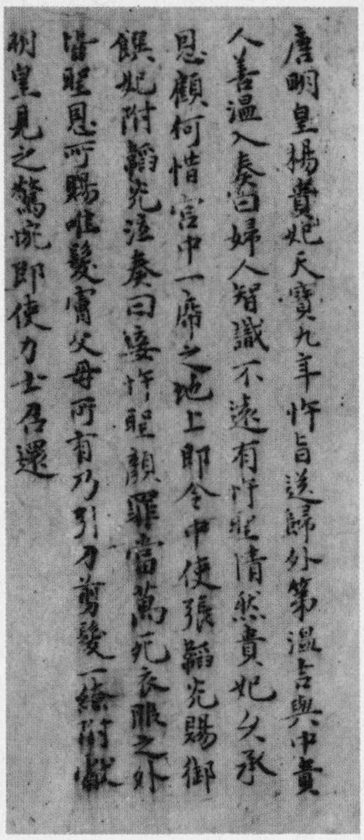

In 1644 the Ming empire was conquered by a tribe of northern warriors, the Manchus. The new rulers of China adopted many of the traditions of their predecessors, including the sacrosanct isolation of the emperor within the walls of the Forbidden City. Evert Ides, a representative of Tsar Peter the Great of Russia, was one of the few seventeenth-century foreigners who breached those walls by means of diplomacy and proffered gifts.

On the twelfth of November the *Viceroy* sent some *Mandaryns* to give me notice to appear with their Czarish Majesties Credentials next Morning in the Castle; upon which I accordingly prepared myself. At eight in the Morning three principal *Mandaryns* came to advise me that it was then a proper time to wait on the Emperour. Besides their common Habit, they were also dressed in Robes, which were Embroidered some with Dragons, others with Lyons, and a third sort with Tygers and Cranes on the Breast and Back work'd with Gold Thread. They brought with them 50 Horses for my Retinue. . . .

Coming to the outer Gate of the Castle, there is a Pillar, with some Characters Engraven on it, where I was told I must alight, according to the Custom, so that I went on foot through five outer Courts to the Castle itself. I found a great number of *Mandaryns* at the Court, all clothed in their richest Embroidered Robes, such as they wear in the Emperour's presence, who waited for me.

After we had mutually exchanged Compliments, the Emperour appeared on his Throne; upon which I delivered their Czarish Majesties Credentials, and after the usual Ceremonies and a short Speech, was conducted back.

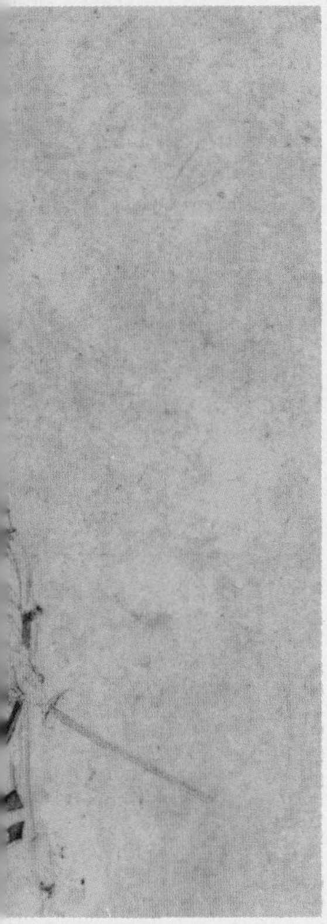

On the sixteenth of the same Month, I was informed that I was invited to Eat before the Emperour: wherefore in the Morning accompanied with the *Mandaryns* thereto appointed, and the chief Gentlemen of my Retinue, I rode to Court. And in the sixth Court, a great many Lords and *Mandaryns* were standing in rows in their best Robes, and shortly after an order came down for us to appear above in the Palace. As soon as I entered, the Emperour mounted his exalted Throne, having near him some Persons who play'd very finely on the Fife, and a Life-Guard of twelve men with Gilt Halberds without any sharp point to them, but adorned with Leopards and Tygers-Tails. As soon as the King was seated, the Musick ceased, and the Halberdiers seated themselves cross legged on each side below the Throne. The Emperour's Table was furnished with Cold Meats, Fruits and Sweet-Meats, served up in Silver Dishes, and the whole covered with yellow Damask. . . .

The Palace is an oblong Quadrangular Brick building, which is twice as long as broad, and the Roof covered with yellow glazed Tiles, on which were fixed Lyons, Dragons and all sorts of Imagery. . . . the Ascent to the Hall was up several Steps, and the farther part or entrance of it was provided with small open places or Windows, which were not glazed but peaked with Paper. At the ends of this Hall were two Doors, the tops of which were adorned with a sort of carved work, somewhat like a Crown, which was extraordinarily well gilt. This building hath neither any Room over it nor arched Roof, but the height of the Room is to the very top of the Roof, which was composed of various Pannels, beautifully coloured, Japanned and finely gilded. . . .

The Throne is placed opposite to the Eastern Entrance, against the hind Wall, and is about three Fathoms broad, and as many long; before it are two

Ascents with six Steps each, adorned with Rails and cast representations of Leaves very well gilt. On the right and left sides were also Rails of cast Imagery, which some report to be Gold, and others Silver; which are also extraordinarily well gilt. Exactly in the middle of this raised place is a Throne somewhat like an Altar, which opens with two Doors; and in it the Emperour's seat about an ell high, covered with black Sables, on which he sate with his Legs across under him. This Monarch was then Aged about 50 Years, his Meen was very agreeable, he had large black Eyes, and his Nose was somewhat raised; he wore small black *Mustachio's*, but had very little or no Beard on the lower part of his Face; he was very much pitted with the Small Pox, and of a middling Stature. His Dress consisted of a common dark-colour'd Damask Waistcoat, a Coat of deep blue Sattin, adorn'd with Ermins, besides which he had a String of Coral hanging about his Neck, and down on his Breast. He had a warm Cap on turned up with Sable, to which was added a red Silk Knot, and some Peacocks Feathers hanging down backwards. His Hair, plaited into one Lock, hung behind him. He had no Gold nor Jewels about him. He had Boots on, which were made of black Velvet.

Whilst he was at Dinner, such an orderly and profound Silence was observed amongst the *Mandaryns*, that not only no Noise was heard, but they forbore so much as speaking to one another, all sitting very still with modest down-cast Eyes.

EVERT YSBRAND IDES
Travels Over Land from Muscovy to China, 1706

DOMAIN OF THE EMPRESS DOWAGER

During the nineteenth century the uneasy détente between the Middle Kingdom and the Western nations repeatedly erupted into armed conflict. In 1900 a government-sanctioned secret society, the Boxers, attacked the foreign legations in Peking in a desperate attempt to eradicate the "barbarians." In retaliation, an international expedition occupied the capital, forcing the empress dowager and the emperor to flee. The deserted Forbidden City became the scene of wanton looting by rapacious soldiers. Among the more dignified visitors was a French naval officer, the novelist Pierre Loti.

I wanted to see the Violet City and its throne rooms once more before going away, and to enter it this time, not by round-about ways and back doors and secret posterns, but by the great avenues and gates that have been for centuries closed, so that I might try to imagine beneath the destruction of to-day what must have been in former times the splendor of the sovereigns' arrival.

No one of our European capitals has been conceived and laid out with such unity and audacity, with the idea of increasing the magnificence of a pageant always dominant, especially that of imparting an imposing effect to the appearance of the Emperor. . . . It is easy to understand why the Chinese ambassadors, who came to visit our kings in the times when their immense country was flourishing, were not particularly dazzled by the sight of the Paris of those days, of the Louvre or of Versailles. . . .

Things must have begun to go to pieces here centuries ago; the red plaster of the walls has fallen in places, or it has become spotted with black; the marble of the obelisks and the great squinting lions could only have grown so yellow under the rains of innumerable seasons, and the green that pushes through wherever the granite is joined, marks with lines of velvet the design of the pavement.

The last triple gates, given over since the defeat to a detachment of American soldiers, will open to-day for any barbarian, such as I, who carries a properly signed permit.

Passing through the tunnels, one enters an immense marble whiteness, — a whiteness that is turning into ivory yellow and is stained by the autumn leaves and the wild growth that has invaded this deserted spot. The place is paved with marble, and straight ahead, rising like a wall, is an extraordinary marble terrace, on which stands the throne room, with its sturdy blood-red columns and its roof of old enamel. This white enclosure is like a cemetery — so much green has pushed its way up between the paving-stones, — where the silence is broken only by the magpies and the crows. . . .

One mounts to [the] terraces by staircases of Babylonian proportions and by an "imperial path," reserved for the Emperor alone, that is to say, by an inclined plane made of one block of marble, — one of those untransportable blocks which men in the past possessed the secret of moving. The five-clawed dragon displays his sculptured coils from the top to the bottom of this stone, which cuts the big white staircase into two equal parts, of which it forms the centre, and extends right to the foot of the throne. No Chinese would dare to walk on this "path" by which the emperors descend, pressing the high soles of their shoes on the scales of the heraldic beast, in order not to slip.

The room at the top, open to-day to all the winds that blow and to all the birds of heaven, has, by way of roof, the most prodigious mass of yellow faience that there is in Pekin, and the most bristling with monsters; the ornaments at the corners are shaped like big extended wings. Inside, needless to say, there is that blaze of reddish gold which always pursues one in Chinese palaces. On the ceiling, which is of an intricate design, dragons are everywhere entwined, entangled, interwoven; their claws and their horns appear, mingled with the clouds, and one of them, which is detached from the mass and seems ready to fall, holds in his hanging jaw a gold sphere directly above the throne. The throne, which is of red and gold lacquer, rises in the centre of this shadowy place on a sort of platform; two large screens made of feathers, emblems of sovereignty, stand behind it, and along the steps which lead up to it are incense-burners similar to those placed in pagodas at the feet of the gods.

Like the avenues through which I have come, like the series of bridges and the triple gates, this throne is in the exact centre of Pekin, and represents its soul; were it not for all these walls, all these various enclosures, the Emperor, seated there on this pedestal of lacquer and marble, could see to the farthest extremities of the city, to the farthest openings in the surrounding walls; the tributary sovereigns who come there, the ambassadors, the armies, from the moment of their entrance into Pekin by the southern gate, would be, so to speak, under the inspiration of his invisible eyes. . . .

The incomprehensible fact about this palace, to us uninitiated barbarians, is that there are three of these rooms exactly alike, with the same throne, the same carpet, the same ornaments, in the same places; they are preceded by the same great marble courts and are constructed on the same marble terraces; you reach them by the same staircases and by the same imperial paths.

Why should there be three of them? For, of necessity, the first conceals the two others, and in order to pass from the first to the second, or from the second to the third, you must go down each time into a vast gloomy court without any view and then come up again between the piles of ivory-colored marble, so superb, yet so monotonous and oppressive! . . .

I had already seen the private apartments of the young Emperor. Those of the Empress — for she had apartments here too, in addition to the frail palaces her fancy had scattered over the parks of the Yellow City — those of the Empress are less gloomy and much less dark. Room after room exactly alike, with large windows and superb yellow enamelled roofs. Each one has its marble steps, guarded by two lions all shining with gold, and the little gardens which separate them are filled with bronze ornaments, heraldic beasts, phoenixes, or crouching monsters.

Inside are yellow silks and square arm-chairs of the form consecrated by time, unchanging as China itself. On the chests, on the tables, a quantity of precious articles are placed in small glass cases, — because of the perpetual dust of Pekin, — and this makes them as cheerless as mummies and casts over the apartment the chill of a museum. There are many artificial bouquets of chimerical flowers of neutral shades in amber, jade, agate, and moonstones. . . .

Behind the sleeping-room of the Empress a kind of dark oratory is filled with Buddhistic divinities on altars. An exquisite odor still remains, left behind her by the beautiful, passionate, elegant old woman who was queen. Among these gods is a small creature made of very old wood, quite worn and dull from the loss of gilding, who wears about his neck a collar of fine pearls. In front of him is a bunch of dried flowers, — a last offering, one of the guardian eunuchs informs me, made by the Empress to this little old Buddha, who was her favorite fetish, at the supreme moment before her flight from the Violet City.

To-day I have reached this retreat by a very different route from the one I took on my first pilgrimage here, and in going out I must now pass through the quarters where all is walled and rewalled, the gates barricaded and guarded by more and more horrible monsters. Are there hidden princesses and treasures here? There is always the same bloody color on the walls, the same yellow faience on the roofs, and more horns, claws, cruel forms, hyena smiles, projecting teeth, and squinting eyes than ever; the most unimportant things, like bolts and locks, have features that simulate hatred and death.

Everything is perishing from old age; the stones are worn away, the wooden doors are falling into dust. There are some old shadowy courts that are given up to white-bearded octogenarian servants, who have built cabins, where they live like recluses, occupied in training magpies or in cultivating sickly flowers in pots under the eyes of the everlasting grinning old marble and bronze beasts. No cloistered green, no monk's cell, was ever half so gloomy as these little courts, so shut in and so dark, overshadowed for centuries by the uncontrolled caprices of the Chinese emperors. The inexorable sentence, "Leave hope behind, all those who enter here," seems to belong here; as one proceeds, the passages grow narrower and more intricate; it seems as though there were no escape, as though the great locks on the doors would refuse to work, as though the walls would close in upon and crush you.

Yet here I am almost outside, outside the interior wall and through the massive gates that quickly close behind me. Now I am between the second rampart and the first, both equally terrible. I am on the road which makes a circle around this city, — a sort of ominous passageway of great length that runs between two dark red walls and which seems to meet in the distance ahead of me. Human bones and old rags that have been parts of the clothing

144

of soldiers are scattered here and there, and one sees two or three crows and one of the flesh-eating dogs prowling about.

When the boards which barricade the outside gate are let down for me (the gate guarded by the Japanese), I discover, as though on awakening from a dreadful dream, that I am in the park of the Yellow City, in open space under the great cedars.

PIERRE LOTI
The Last Days of Pekin, 1902

Shortly after the signing of the Boxer Protocol in 1902, the empress dowager and her court were permitted to return to Peking. The wily "Old Buddha," who for forty years had been the effective ruler of China and a fierce opponent of all things foreign, immediately adopted a policy of reconciliation. Among Tz'u Hsi's innovations were frequent audiences in the Forbidden City for the ladies of the diplomatic corps. Lady Susan Townley, the wife of a high-ranking official in the British Embassy, recorded her impressions of one such occasion.

It may be imagined with what interest I went to the first audience which the Empress-Dowager gave to the ladies of the Corps Diplomatique after my arrival in Peking. We were invited to the Winter Palace which lies in the heart of the Forbidden City. As I was rapidly carried in an official sedan chair past so many now historic spots, my impression was one of numberless great courtyards succeeding each other and connected by Chinese gateways decorated with dragons and other devices. . . .

As we approached the Holy of Holies our official chairs were forbidden to penetrate further and we had to alight and take our places in Palace chairs upholstered in red satin and slung upon two poles, in which we were carried by imperial bearers through further courtyards and gates to the Great Hall of Audience. This hall is built on a raised terrace of white marble and is approached by a noble flight of steps, at the foot of which were grouped, waiting for us, a gorgeous company of mandarins, court ladies and attendants.

It was a grateful moment when we passed from the glare of a blazing midday sun into the cool atmosphere and subdued light of the throne-room, in the centre of which stood a huge vase holding a block of solid ice to cool the air. Exactly opposite the door by which we entered sat the Empress-Dowager. In front of her was a high table covered with yellow silk on which were set two vases filled with chrysanthemums, and between them a glass case containing a carved coral sceptre of exquisite workmanship. It was not until the Empress-Dowager pushed aside this glass case, in order to stretch forward and shake hands across the table with the ladies who were presented to her, that I had an opportunity of really studying this remarkable woman of whom I have heard and read so much. She sat upon a kind of Turkish divan covered with figured chinese silk of a beautiful yolk of egg colour; being low of stature, her feet (which are of natural size, she being a Manchu) barely touched the ground, and only her head and shoulders were visible over the table placed in front of her. She wore a Chinese coat, loose and hanging from the shoulders, of a diaphanous pale blue silk material covered with the most exquisite Chinese embroidery of vine leaves and grapes. Round her neck was a pale blue satin ribbon about an inch and a half wide, studded with large lustrous pearls, pierced, and sewn to the ribbon. Her head was dressed according to the Manchu fashion, the hair being parted in front and brushed smoothly over the ears, to be afterwards caught up at the back and draped high and wide over a kind of paper-cutter of dark green jade set, like an Alsatian bow, crosswise on the summit of the head. The ends of this paper-cutter were decorated with great bunches of artificial flowers, butterflies and hanging crimson silk tassels. Her complexion is that of a North Italian and being a widow her cheeks are unpainted and unpowdered according to Chinese custom in such cases. Her piercing dark eyes when not engaged looking at the ladies roved curiously about amongst her surroundings. Her age is sixty-eight as she told us herself, but her hair being dyed jet black and most of it artificial her appearance is that of a much younger woman. Her hands are long and tapering and like those of many Chinese women very prettily shaped, but they are disfigured by the curious national custom of letting the nails grow inordinately long. The nails of the two smaller fingers of the right hand were protected by gold shields which fitted to the finger like a lady's thimble and gradually tapered off to a length of three or four inches. . . .

. . . As each foreign lady was presented the Empress-Dowager leant forward and graciously shook hands with her. Where has she learnt the ease and dignity with which she receives her European guests? The formal presentation over, she rose and signified, through an interpreter, that we should now be conducted through the various apartments of the Palace to the banqueting hall, where a repast had been prepared for us. In Chinese houses each apartment is separated from the other by an open court. The Empress-Dowager therefore left the throne-room and took her place in a yellow silk carrying-chair which was borne by twelve eunuchs, a thirteenth holding a yellow silk umbrella over the imperial head! . . .

At last we came to the Banqueting Hall and here the most curious sight of all awaited us. In this essentially Chinese hall with its dragon-ornamented gallery and painted columns stood a long table and rows of ordinary European dining-room chairs. They were evidently procured for our special comfort, but they looked strangely tawdry and out of place in their present surroundings. An ordinary cloth was spread upon the table, but in order to preserve its whiteness immaculate it was covered with shiny American oil-cloth, the ground of which was black, besprigged with coloured flowers. The centre of the table was laden with countless dishes of Chinese dainties and before each place was set a European knife, spoon and fork of inferior metal, besides also a set of blackwood silver-mounted chop-sticks. To each of us was also given a napkin (hailing evidently from Manchester) of coarse cotton, mauve in colour and adorned with a large white floral design. The fare was Chinese, the liquor consisted of tepid beer poured into a wine glass, or champagne in liqueur glasses! Needless to say we did not eat much, although the Empress-Dowager who sat at our table was most anxious that we should do so, and herself set us an example by consuming several bowlsful of rice and milk, a great mark of favour, for she never sits at the same table as her court ladies and always eats in private. On this occasion she was served by kneeling attendants and used imperial yellow china; our dishes were yellow with green and black dragons on them. Later in the day we were given the napkins, chop-sticks, and dishes out of which we had eaten, also the Chinese "menu" as souvenirs of the occasion!

LADY SUSAN TOWNLEY
My Chinese Note Book, 1904

Apart from the emperor, only eunuchs and women were privileged to reside within the Forbidden City. In 1903 the Princess Der Ling, the Western-educated daughter of a member of the Manchu White Banner Corps, received the high honor of appointment as lady-in-waiting to the empress dowager.

One day Her Majesty suggested that she should show us round the Forbidden City. First we proceeded to the Audience Hall. This differs somewhat from the Audience Hall of the Summer Palace. To enter, one must mount some twenty odd steps of white marble, with rails on either side of the steps made of the same material. At the top of the steps a large veranda, supported by huge pillars of wood, painted red, surrounded the building. The windows along this verandah were of marvellously carved trellis-work, designed to represent the character "Shou" arranged in different positions. Then we entered the hall itself. The floor is of brick, and Her Majesty told us that all these bricks were of solid gold and had been there for centuries. They were of a peculiar black color, doubtless painted over, and were so slippery that it was most difficult to keep on one's feet. The furnishing was similar to that in the Audience Halls in the Summer Palace and in the Sea Palace, with the exception that the throne was made of dark brown wood inlaid with jade of different colors.

The Hall was only used for audience on very rare occasions, such as the birthday of the Empress Dowager and New Year's Day, and no foreigner has ever entered this building. All the usual audiences were held in a smaller building in the Forbidden City.

After spending some little time in the Audience Hall, we next visited the Emperor's quarters. These were much smaller than those occupied by Her Majesty, but were very elaborately furnished. There were thirty-two rooms, many of which were never used, but all were furnished in the same expensive style. In the rear of this building was the Palace of the Young Empress, which was smaller still, having about twenty-four rooms in all, and in the same building three rooms were set apart for the use of the Secondary Wife of the Emperor. Although close together, the Palaces of the Emperor and his wife were not connected by any entrance, but both buildings were surrounded by verandas connecting with Her Majesty's apartments, which were quite a distance away. There were several other buildings, which were used as waiting-rooms for visitors. In addition to the above, there were several buildings which were not used at all; these were sealed and nobody seemed to know what they contained, or whether they contained anything at all. Even Her Majesty said she had never been inside these buildings, as they had been sealed for many years. Even the entrance to the enclosure containing these buildings was always closed, and this was the only occasion that any of us ever even passed through. They were quite different in appearance from any other buildings in the Palace, being very dirty and evidently of great age. We were commanded not to talk about the place at all.

The apartments of the Court ladies were connected with those of Her Majesty, but the rooms were so small one could hardly turn round in them; also they were very cold in winter. The servants' quarters were at the end of our apartments, but there was no entrance and they could only be reached by passing along our veranda, while the only entrance we ourselves had to our rooms was by passing along Her Majesty's veranda. This was Her Majesty's own idea, in order that she could keep an eye on all of us and could see when we either went out or came in.

Her Majesty now conducted us to her own Palace, and pausing a little said: "I will now show you something which will be quite new to you." We entered a room adjoining her bedroom, which was connected by a narrow passage some fifteen feet in length. On either side the walls were painted and decorated very beautifully. Her Majesty spoke to one of the eunuch attendants, who stooped down and removed from the ground at each end of this passage two wooden plugs which were fitted into holes in the basement. I then began to realize that what I had hitherto regarded as solid walls were in reality sliding panels of wood. These panels when opened revealed a kind of grotto. There were no windows, but in the roof was a skylight. At one end of this room or grotto was a large rock, on the top of which was a seat with a yellow cushion, and beside the cushion an incense burner. Everything had the appearance of being very old. The room contained no furniture of any description. One end of this room led into another passage similar to the one already described, having sliding panels, which led into another grotto, and so on; in fact the whole of the palace walls were intersected by these secret passages, each concealing an inner room. Her Majesty told us that during the Ming dynasty these rooms had been used for various purposes, principally by the Emperor when he wished to be alone. One of these secret rooms was used by Her Majesty as a treasure room where she kept her valuables. During the time of the Boxer trouble, she hid all her valuables here before she fled. When she returned and opened this secret room she found everything intact, not one of the vandals who ransacked the Palace even suspecting there was such a place.

We returned to our veranda, and on looking around for the rooms we had just vacated, could see nothing excepting black stone walls, so well were they hidden. One of the principal reasons for Her Majesty's dislike to the Forbidden City was the mysteries which it contained, many of which she did not know of herself. She said: "I don't even talk about these places at all, as people might think that they were used for all kinds of purposes."

THE PRINCESS DER LING
Two Years in the Forbidden City, 1911

Upon the deaths of both the emperor and the empress dowager in 1908, the last of the Manchus, two-year-old P'u-yi, ascended the dragon throne. Although the boy-emperor was forced to abdicate three years later by the leaders of the newly established republic, he was allowed to live on in the Forbidden City, which was maintained as an anachronistic imperial enclave. One touch of modernity was the appointment of Reginald Johnston, a distinguished English professor, as tutor.

THE LAST MANCHU

The years of my service in the Forbidden City may be regarded as having been divided into two periods. The first was from March, 1919, to November, 1922, and closed with the emperor's marriage. The second was from the latter date to that of his summary expulsion, in November, 1924, from the palace which had been his home since infancy. . . .

Throughout the earlier period [the emperor] attended daily at the Yü-ch'ing Kung ("Palace of the Bringing-Forth of Blessings") which had been the imperial study or schoolroom for many years. It was the private residence of the emperor Chia-Ch'ing (1796–1820) after he had been nominated heir-apparent, and it contains autograph scrolls by him. It had a gateway of its own which led into a small courtyard. In the courtyard, to the left of the gate, was a waiting-room for the exclusive use of the tutors. A staff of servants (known by the Manchu term *sula*) had the sole duty of waiting upon them and serving them with tea from ever-ready and inexhaustible sources. The main building faced eastwards, at right angles to the waiting room. Each tutor entered the Forbidden City by the Gate of Spiritual Valour, or, if more convenient to himself, by the Gate of Eastern or the Gate of Western Glory. Leaving his car or carriage outside the gate (I was the only one of the tutors who used a car in preference to a pony-carriage) he was carried through the gate in his official chair, acknowledging, as he went, the salute of the armed sentries. I was again alone among the tutors in occasionally exercising my alternative right to ride into the Forbidden City on horseback. On arrival at one of the inner gates — that known as the Ching-yün Mên — the tutor's chair was set down, or he dismounted from his horse, and the short remaining distance to the Yü-ch'ing palace was traversed on foot.

The tutor sat in the waiting-room, sipping tea, until the arrival of the emperor. He came in an enormous palanquin draped in yellow silk and carried by twelve or more bearers. As it entered the courtyard, etiquette forbade the tutor to go out and meet him. But he rose from his seat and stood in the waiting-room (though it was impossible for him to be seen by the emperor) until his majesty had entered the schoolroom. The tutor then resumed his seat until a loud cry of *chao* (a word denoting the imperial summons) uttered by a eunuch at the door of the main building, and repeated by one of the *sula*, announced that his majesty was ready to begin his studies.

The tutor immediately entered the schoolroom and bowed once in the direction of his pupil who was standing at the north side of a square table. Both then sat down simultaneously, the tutor's seat being at right angles to that of the emperor, who sat facing the south. . . .

During the first few weeks of my tutorship I was not allowed to be alone with the emperor. There was always a solitary eunuch in attendance; and we were also joined either by one of the Chinese tutors, usually Chu I-fan, or by one of the ministers of the household, usually Ch'i-Ling. The eunuch stood motionless against the wall; the tutor or minister sat with us at the table, facing north. The reason given for the presence of the latter was that his majesty, never having spoken to a foreigner before, might feel nervous or embarrassed. Of nervousness, however, I detected no sign; and when our companion showed obvious signs of somnolence, which happened almost daily, the emperor made no attempt to wake him up or to remind him that his function was to keep a sleepless eye on the barbarian from overseas whose innocent appearance might be the cloak of a black heart.

Before the second month had elapsed the emperor was assumed to have recovered from whatever nervousness or embarrassment he felt at first in his foreign tutor's presence, and the Chinese tutor or minister ceased to give us the pleasure of his company. The eunuch, however, remained. . . .

The eunuch stood in silence just inside the doorway. At the end of half an hour he made a noiseless exit, and another equally silent (and shoeless) eunuch took his place. This one was, in his turn, relieved by a third. The process was repeated every half hour.

REGINALD F. JOHNSTON
Twilight in the Forbidden City, 1934

If I was at all interested when the princes told me on the orders of the High Consorts that I was old enough for my "Grand Nuptials" it was because marriage would mark my coming of age and would mean that others could no longer control me as if I were still a child.

The people who felt most concern over the matter were the old ladies. Early in 1921, when I was just fifteen, the High Consorts summoned my father for a number of consultations on the subject and then called a meeting of about ten of the princes to discuss it. Almost two years later the wedding took place. . . .

In the last resort the choice had to be made by the "emperor". The way that this had been done in the time of Tung Chih and Kuang Hsu was for the girls who were candidates to stand in a line and the future bridegroom to select one of them. I have heard two versions of how he indicated his choice. One was that he handed a jade symbol to the girl who took his fancy; the other was that he hung a pouch on the girl's buckle. When it came to my time the princes felt that lining up a row of maidens would no longer be suitable and decided that I should choose from photographs instead. I was to pencil a mark on the picture of the one I liked best.

Four photos were sent to the Mind Nurture Palace. To me the girls seemed much the same and their bodies looked as shapeless as tubes in their dresses. Their faces were very small in the pictures so that I could not see whether they were beauties or not. The only comparison I could make was between the styles of their clothes. It did not occur to me at the time that this was one of the great events of my life, and I had no standards to guide me. I casually drew a circle on a pretty picture.

She was the daughter of Tuan Kung of the Manchu Ordet clan. She was called Wen Hsiu (her other name was Hui Hsin) and she was three years younger than me, so that she would have been twelve when I saw her picture. . . .

From the entry into the palace of the trousseau of the consort to the ceremony at which I received congratulations in the Cloudless Heaven Palace the wedding lasted five days. The celebrations included three days of theatricals and the granting of new titles.

What caused the most public indignation was that after the attempted restoration in 1917 the little court was flaunting its pomp outside the Forbidden City. The ceremonial emblems of the Ching court were paraded with great majesty round the streets of Peking under the respectful protection of large numbers of Republican soldiers and police. On the day of the wedding ceremony proper two princes dressed in Ching court robes with staffs of office in their hands rode on horseback behind two Republican military bands. They were followed by more army bands and cavalry, mounted police, and mounted security police. After them came seventy-two dragon-and-phoenix parasols and flags, four "yellow pavilions" (containing the imperial patent for the new empress and her clothing), and thirty pairs of palace lanterns. This imposing procession set out for the "Residence of the Empress". . . .

The rich presents given by leading figures of the Republic also attracted considerable attention. President Li Yuan-hung wrote "Offering of President Li Yuan-hung of the Republic of China to the Hsuan Tung Emperor" on a red card and gave the following presents: four vessels in cloisonné, two kinds of silk and satin, one curtain and a pair of scrolls wishing me longevity, prosperity and good fortune. Ex-President Hsu Shih-chang sent 20,000 dollars and many other valuable presents including twenty-eight pieces of porcelain and a sumptuous Chinese carpet with a dragon and phoenix design. Chang Tso-lin, Wu Pei-fu, Chang Hsun, Tsao Kun and other warlords and politicians also sent cash and many other kinds of presents.

The representative of the Republic at the ceremony, Yin Chang, was a chief aide-de-camp in the Office of the President, and he congratulated me formally as he would have done a foreign sovereign. When he had finished bowing to me he announced, "That was on behalf of the Republic. Your slave will now greet Your Majesty in his private capacity." With this he knelt on the floor and kotowed to me.

At the time many papers severely criticized these strange occurrences but this did nothing to dampen the enthusiasm of the princes and high officials, nor did it prevent veterans of the Ching from emerging all over the country like insects waking up after the winter and converging on Peking in swarms. They brought presents that included money and antiques from themselves and others. The valuables were not as important, however, as the power that the court now seemed to enjoy, which went beyond even their own expectations and made them feel that our prospects were very hopeful.

What caused the High Consorts, princes, high officials and veterans of the Ching the most excitement was the presence of guests from the Legation Quarter. This was the first time that foreign officials had appeared in the Forbidden City since the Revolution of 1911, and although they came in their personal capacities they were still, after all, foreign officials.

AISIN-GIORO P'U-YI
From Emperor to Citizen, 1964

LITERARY IMPRESSIONS

By 1916 the ill-fated republic had disintegrated into anarchy. Years of civil war among competing warlords and, later, between Communist and Nationalist forces, left northern China vulnerable to Japanese aggression — and in 1937 Peking itself was taken. But even under Japanese occupation, the ancient charm of the city continued to lure Europeans, such as the English poet Osbert Sitwell.

Across the first and greatest of the courts, runs down its marble channel in a wide and most delicate curve, the celebrated canal, Golden Water River, with three fine marble bridges crossing it. To me, for one, observing this prodigious enclosure, it always seemed that, in the fortress-like grandeur of the edifice behind, in the line of the canal and the poetry of its waters, flickering reflected sunlight under perfect spans, in the workmanship and design of the balustrades, in the vista of lofty, superb halls in front, with their scarlet and green eaves high in air, and still above, in the vista of roofs fitting, one into another, with supreme art, the Palace reached its culmination. The theme is one of ascent, flowing and progressive from flight of steps to flight of steps, from terrace to terrace, from lower deck to upper deck, from one building to another. The similarity and slight difference between court and court, roof and roof, outline and outline, invests it with the depth and immensity of a night sky when, gazing at it, you try to identify a single star. Yet each court constitutes a world of its own, remote in feeling as the moon; a world wherein nothing happens except the ceaseless, clock-like sweep of cold, golden light from east to west, across it, across the marble floors, across the broad and shallow flights of steps, across the canal, lying like a scimitar below, across the cracking, sagging terraces, their surface dry and powdery with age.

. . . the Chinese is the only fully developed system of polychrome architecture extant: no other (though many have done so in the past, Greek and Gothic among them) now relies upon colour for a full half of its effect. The European is the art of mass and contrast, Chinese that of harmony and balance. . . . here court opens out of court, hall out of hall, united by a marked symphonic similarity. It is an art of suave and subtle modulation, intensely civilised and well-bred, as against one of opposition. The risk — as a rule triumphantly avoided — which through its very nature Chinese architecture incurs, is of monotony; that to which European is liable, of extravagance. The Chinese buildings aspire to the same extent, but are humbler in that they do not attempt the soaring ambition of Gothic, or the gesticulations, the rhetorical questions to Heaven, of Baroque. In another respect, as well, Chinese architecture strives less. It does not, as we do, build for eternity. . . . Soaring, thousand-year-old towers of carved stone or reinforced concrete — as though even stone by itself did not afford a sufficient chance of survival — are alien in spirit to the Chinese builder (though modern circumstances may oblige him temporarily to use a medium foreign to him). On the contrary, he accepts fate; fires, earthquakes, plundering by armies and the massacres they recurrently inflict; and plans his edifices so that, when they have been burned down — which, the experience of four thousand years has taught him, happens every hundred years or so — they can very easily and precisely be repeated, and will seem, on the contrary, never to have been injured. (Indeed, a notable fault of Chinese architecture, as well as a notable merit, . . . consists in its transience: it can disappear, melt into nothingness as easily as, on the other hand, it can be renewed.) Thus the great reverence which the Chinese possess — or until lately possessed — for antiquity in a building, comes from a knowledge of how difficult it is for any building to achieve it: and this also explains a little, I think, the occasional surprising want of accurate knowledge on the part of the Chinese connoisseur concerning the date of some of his most admired and precious temples. . . . It is very old — or it looks very old: both are the same to him. And should a building truly prove to be of great age, he is agreeably surprised. . . . So would he regard the Palace; it looks very old, it is very old. . . .

A tragic air broods in these bright, cold courts, fanned by arctic winds and yet so much sadder for the warmth and light of this sun, which, enclosed after this fashion by stone and marble, contrives to impart a certain heat, enough to make the blood thaw from the heart of winter. And in each hall, with its tall, red columns and gold ceiling and coloured walls, broods a painted, gilded and shimmering-eyed beauty, like that of a peacock's tail, in which the Manchu Emperors seem still angrily to live and move, as might a wasp in the heart of a ripe nectarine.

OSBERT SITWELL
Escape with Me!, 1939

The long and violent struggle between the Communists and the Nationalists was finally resolved in 1949 with the establishment of the People's Republic of China, under the leadership of Mao Tse-tung, and the flight to Taiwan of Chiang Kai-shek and his followers. When the French novelist Simone de Beauvoir journeyed to Peking six years later, the Communists had transformed the Forbidden City into a public park and museum complex.

You find yourself in the outer courtyard of the Imperial Palace — it is thus the Chinese refer to it today, denying it that fine title, "The Forbidden City," which used to inspire dreamy thoughts in Western visitors. The Chinese are right; if the idea of a forbidden city intrigues, beckons, it is because of a contradiction in terms: a city into which the population is not admitted has obviously usurped the title of a city. It was nothing but their pride that enabled the old emperors to suppose that their presence in the place they inhabited raised it to the rank of a city; as a matter of fact, their city was never anything beyond a palace. To it they gave yet another gorgeous name: The Violet-Purple City. Here too disappointment awaits the over-credulous traveler. The enclosing walls and the inside walls are of a somewhat drab red bordering on the color of brick. Actually, the "violet-purple" epithet designated not a visible hue but a symbolic one. . . .

Within the walls courtyards and marble terraces supporting gilt-roofed pavilions extend one after the other for more than half a mile; the main buildings trace the central axis; on either side lesser buildings are disposed asymmetrically. At the far end are "The Palace of Cloudless Heaven" given over to the Emperor and "The Palace of Earthly Peace" where the Empress lived. The terraces, for which the marble was brought from the Burmese frontiers on the backs of elephants, are surrounded by gleaming white sculptured balustrades, influenced probably by Hindu art. The buildings are purely Chinese. They are similar to clay models of ancient houses found in tombs dating back several thousand years. Their most remarkable feature is their roofs, characterized — as in the imitations everybody is familiar with — by their steep pitch, their jutting edges, their upturned corners; they are covered with half-cylindrical tiles whose golden glaze glows more than shines. Processions of fabulous animals extend downward along the angles, or hips, of the roofs — owls and dragons symbolizing imperial virtues — at the edges of the gutters other fantastic creatures are there to drink the waters from heaven and prevent floods. . . .

It affects me more strongly if instead of the buildings I turn my attention to the spaces they delimit: courtyards, terraces, stairways. As in certain modern private houses and developments an ambivalence between the ideas of outside and inside is reflected here; this porch was only meant to be a thoroughfare, that court was a ballroom where people stood for hours on end. One must not, therefore, consider this parvis, these tiered gardens as mere devices for setting edifices in perspective; they constitute architectural objects in themselves; their proportions, their dimensions, symmetry subtly played against asymmetry, the solemn quality of the stairways, the balustrades' gracefulness compel admiration. Here, I feel, is where the imperial architects won their outstanding success: in imparting this movement to space, where, with stately, gradual rhythms, pauses and ascents are ordered with the sure mastery that also prescribes oblique promenades in the maze of lateral alleys and sequestered walks.

153

All the same, this beauty strikes me as chill, and I know why. There is nothing accidental about the impermanence of the materials; it is simultaneously the cause, the effect, the expression of a troubling fact: the traces left upon this palace by the past are so few that, paradoxically, I would hesitate to call it a historical monument; it was, like Peking, begun anew by each dynasty: it preserves the mark of none of them. Versailles — that is Louis XIV; and the Escorial is Philip II; whatever else they may be — stirring, detestable, awe-inspiring — the ghosts haunting the castles of Europe are distinctive. Here, nothing conjures up Kublai, Yung Lo, or Ch'ien Lung. One has the feeling this inner city never really belonged to them, that they never belonged to it — in all likelihood because they never belonged to themselves. Between the encroachments of their private debauches and the sacred character of their public office, they were too hemmed in to affirm their personalities; those who may have possessed such a thing frittered it away in this enclave, estranged from their mandate and seeking oblivion in pleasure; that is why the hot-blooded barbarian conquerors found Peking so boring. The only shade lingering still in the phoenix-and-dragon-adorned apartments is that of "the Old Buddha," the Empress Tzu Hsi, and she scarcely fires one's imagination. This palace, in which not one dated memory is inscribed, strikes me as the unalterable seat of an unalterable institution and not the dwelling place of men who were one time alive. . . .

. . . the Violet-Purple City was alleged to enclose heaven and earth — for, living apart from everybody else, the Son of Heaven was not to be excluded from anywhere — it suggests that the world is an intact, sealed whole, that the inventory of its contents is complete, and that the entire business can be reproduced in a pocket-sized model; it reduces the world to the ludicrous dimensions of somebody's private life; it negates the world. In the entire Imperial Palace there is not a single spot from which one can get a glimpse of Peking. The sultans of the Alhambra exploited their people: but glancing from their window, they used at least to look down with affectionate pride at the city and the rich Vega sprawled out at their feet; and, framed between two alabaster colonnettes, the hills of Granada were guests in the palace. The imperial retreat afforded the Son of Heaven not a point of view upon the world but a rampart protecting his august person from outside contagions. It was edified in order to realize an absolute divorce.

The barriers have tumbled. The Forbidden City has become a public place; now everyone strolls freely through its courtyards, sips tea under its porches; Young Pioneers in red neckerchiefs visit the exhibits mounted in its hallways; certain buildings have been turned into palaces of culture, into libraries; in another part of it the government has its seat. Beneath this new life invading it the original meaning of the palace remains unimpaired; I seldom succeeded in forgetting it. But there was one time when, wandering at random, with nothing of old history or myths in my head, I fell in love with some abandoned secondary courtyards gone to weeds or else planted with little dark trees, infinitely deserted and solitary. In one corner dandelions would be growing; the reddish wall capped by gilt tiles and running along an ill-paved court made me think of farms I have seen in Burgundy. Bucolic, divested of all purpose, this too frequently restored palace speaks in the moving language of ruins.

SIMONE DE BEAUVOIR
The Long March, 1958

唐明皇審羯羷黙然不樂左右曰自韶休入朝陛下無一
日歎何且厭也不遑夫之帝曰吾難春天下肥矣

To another writer who visited Peking in the 1930's, the Forbidden City was an oasis of beauty in an exceedingly troubled world. Nikos Kazantzakis, who later established his international reputation with the publication of Zorba the Greek, *was enchanted by its acres of deserted courtyards and pavilions.*

The little carriage, the ricksha, stopped at the entrance and I stepped down. Vast, mythical, this wonder extended in front of me: wide marble steps, short, fat, laughing bronze lions with heavy bells on their chests like court jesters, all-gold fairy-tale palaces whose kings have become grass, moving lightly on the rooftops. High gates falling apart and marked with three old established words in golden cheerful letters: TAI—CHU—MEN ("Large happy gate"). Gigantic bronze incense burners like caldrons. They are now deserted, without burning coal, without fragrant smoke. In one of these burners I saw a yellow wasp with black stripes weaving the empty cells of her hive. Bronze long-legged storks with high necks, wild marble turtles; and next to the winged imperial dragon was the mythical bird with the long wings, the phoenix, the *feng,* the bird that symbolized the empress. Inside the bronze bird they used to put scents and when the emperor passed by they set them on fire. . . .

The palace where once the harem of the emperor buzzed now shines, surrounded by high, blood-red walls. Hieroglyphic letters appear on the walls like skeletons, like human ribs, like lacerated hands and feet. The rooms are deserted, the walls are peeling and crumbling, the roofs crack, and the yellow, green and blue varnished tiles are breaking loose in fragments. Many large halls have become museums where precious remains of the great treasures are piled up — paintings on silk, earrings, bronze bracelets, fans and small ladies' pillows of porcelain. And on the porcelain are painted weeping women under willow trees. On the shelves are vases with exquisite forms, like breasts, like loins, like necks of women. Tarnished silver mirrors, mortars for cosmetics, green necklaces, a multitude of candles that on a tragic night were extinguished forever.

I pass slowly and let my eyes feast for a long time on the paintings that have remained. Most of them are on silk, others are on wood or fine paper. Beauty, voluptuousness, tenderness. Rivers with slender reeds. Small boats with rambling, wandering women. Tiny full-red flowers at the ends of branches, setting the trees on fire. But this is no fire — only spring. Farther, on a silk fabric, are painted lightly like a dream, like frost, the rocks, the clouds, small villages, short, plump women sitting cross-legged on the grass. A girl holds a basket of flowers and places them at the feet of Buddha and looks at him, begging with tight lips. Why should she speak? He hears her unspoken cries.

A hermit smiles under the wild rocks. Golden pheasants stand like queens and gaze at the endless snow-covered landscape. A light, spiritual intoxication takes hold of you; the mind is elevated, it no longer cries like a peasant, it looks far away to a light, wavy frost, where all the beloved earthly designs are silhouetted, illumined for a moment, and then fade away.

I pass through the grass where once upon a time the famous garden of the harem bloomed, and I discern at the side, amid the thorns, a marble pavilion: this is the bath of the beautiful princess Chsian-Fee. With a dome and low-vaulted doors, it is deserted, without water, full of cobwebs. I wander from palace to palace like a ghost. I caress with my hand the two eternal symbols

155

which are carved everywhere, on the sides of every stairway, high on the tops of every door: the Cloud and the Fire, the symbols of passion and vanity. A flame created all these wonders; it was put out, it became smoke and passed into cloud. Only a soul that remembers and loves can come here and force the cloud to return in its primeval form. "I declare war against time," cries the soul, and turns back the wheel of time, and everything is resurrected. . . .

Throughout the day, wandering like a ghost in these deserted palaces, I reiterate in my mind the tragic fate that weighed on this unapproachable idol, full of responsibility. His person was so sacred that he could not come in contact with his people. He lived isolated, a holy prisoner in his court, and his every act was regulated according to the strictest protocol: in the spring, he lived in the eastern palace, wearing green clothes and eating wheat bread and lamb. In summer, he lived in the southern palace, wearing white clothes and eating dog meat. In winter, he went to the northern palace and wore black clothes and ate pork. The houses were the same color as the emperor's clothes. When he went to offer sacrifice or hunt or wage a war, his carriages were also painted the same color. Thus, imprisoned by inviolable laws, the emperor was a religious puppet who was dressed, washed, scented and transferred from temple to temple. No one was allowed to look in his eyes. One had to bend to look at him and not glance above his neck or below his waist. And when one wanted to talk to him, one had to put before one's mouth a tablet of precious green stone, lest the breath reach him and infect him. . . .

I gather wild flowers and camomiles that sprout on the marble steps. I hear my steps echoing in the deserted rooms of the palace and a superhuman joy buds in my mind. I remember the spring on the island of Crete in the plain of Messara; it is an awesome spectacle: early in the morning, before the sun rises over the plain, sometimes you see high on the dimly lit horizon huge shadows, like an army hastily marching in straight lines. The sun comes out and the armies disappear. The Cretans call these men who are created and disappear with the dew *drosoulites* ("dewlets"). Like them, the Chinese kings passed from the earth and vanished.

NIKOS KAZANTZAKIS
Japan-China, 1963

In August 1967, during the chaotic and turbulent period known as the Cultural Revolution, Anthony Grey, a Reuters correspondent assigned to Peking, was placed under house arrest. The innocent pawn in a Sino-British dispute over Chinese journalists jailed in Hong Kong, he was held in solitary confinement for twenty-six months. Hostage in Peking, Grey's inspiring and remarkably unembittered account of his ordeal, includes an observation of the citizenry's near-worship of Mao Tse-tung at May Day festivities in the capital.

MAO'S PEKING

From my room in the Hsin Chiao (New Bridge) Hotel, I could see workers knocking down the last remaining parts of the great south wall which surrounded the Imperial City of the Chinese Emperors. It was making way for the building of an underground railway, some foreigners said. Others suggested the excavations were for a nuclear blastproof shelter.

Peking in March is cold and whipped by dry, icy winds that bring great clouds of sand with them from the Gobi Desert. During these dust storms everything, both inside and outside the house is covered with a fine layer of grit. The grandeur of the curved golden-tiled roofs of the palaces of the Forbidden City and the broad sweep of the central Boulevard of Eternal Peace cutting through the vast concrete plain of the Square of Heavenly Peace contrast sharply with the drab uniformity of the blue and khaki cotton clothing of the people. . . .

On April 7 Vergil Berger [the former Reuters correspondent] and his wife departed from Peking and I moved from the Hsin Chiao hotel into the two-storey house at 15 Nan Chihtze, under the high grey walls of the Forbidden City. This was to be my home for the next three and a half months and an isolated prison for two further years. . . .

On May 1 I clapped eyes on the living legend that is Mao for the one and only time. And for a brief moment the living face I had seen looking out from a million printed portraits everywhere my glance fell in China did not register, although he was passing within a few feet of me.

It was in the Working People's Palace of Culture standing to the east of the Tien An Men — Gate of Heavenly Peace. There, groves of wistarias, pines, willows, and cypresses surround a group of buildings with yellow-tiled roofs and red walls that were the halls of the Imperial Ancestral Temple in the Ming and Ching dynasties. Now the whole compound is a park with the splendid proletarian name given above.

I went there on the invitation of the Foreign Ministry on May Day morning to watch the cultural displays. Usually on May Day there is no formal parade but Premier Chou En-lai often strolls casually around the parks with a small group of government and party leaders. Mao has normally stayed at home in his single-storied, yellow stone house in another compound adjoining the Forbidden City where the top leadership lives.

But on this morning I noticed that among the crowds, there were thousands of uniformed soldiers of the People's Liberation Army. If I'd had a jot of sense I would have realized immediately why they were there. Perhaps my judgement was affected by the fact that lots of Red Guards, youths and girls, were lining up along the pathways applauding the foreign visitors, including me. I was about to smile back at them when I looked round to check and found I was leading a group of Albanian fraternal friends. But the smiling faces of the Chinese girls were so pleasant I smiled back anyway and clapped back too like the other Communists behind as I walked. It was pleasant to see them looking happy and the sun was shining.

But suddenly the soldiers were moving in a purposeful way. They lined up in ranks three deep along the pathways, linked arms, braced themselves and waited. The crowds behind them thickened in anticipation. And I still expected to see Chou En-lai stroll by.

When the commotion and cheering began out of sight around a bend in the path the penny still didn't drop. And when a jeep rounded the corner into view, for one unenlightened moment I looked at the massively tall, erect figure in high-buttoned grey tunic and cap and thought vaguely "Who's that?"

But the teen-age girls and youths standing around me in the dense crowd didn't wonder. They just went out of their heads. Jumping up and down, screaming, shouting, waving red booklets of the Great Man's quotations. The excited crowd surged in a great rush against the triple barrier of soldiers which bulged forward with the momentum. I was desperately trying to keep my feet in the mêlée. At one time I was practically on my knees, the next being thrust forward in a rush. I had been carrying a tape recorder and the microphone was torn from my hand accidentally and the twelve feet or so of cable wound itself round legs and bodies and I was being hauled around on the end of it. I also had a cine camera, but so great was the commotion as Mao went by, massive, impassive, impressive in his stance, that I never even began to focus it on him.

Suddenly he was gone and the still half-hysterical crowd was streaming after the little convoy of jeeps passing out through the park gates.

Outside the crowd formed up again round the Tien An Men and waited expectantly to see if Mao would make another unexpected, unscheduled appearance. But minutes stretched to half an hour and nothing happened. Then a young handsome Chinese of about eighteen who had been standing quietly in front of me turned and said, to my great surprise in good English "Aren't you English?"

I said I was. Spoken English is rarely encountered in China and I racked my brains for something to say to engage this boy in conversation. Eventually I said rather inanely: "Excuse me but what are you waiting here for?" "To see Chairman Mao, of course," he said and turned back to continue his vigilant watch on the rostrum of the Gate, like the other thousands around me.

"Why?" I persisted.

The boy turned and with a polite expression which contained some pity for one who had to ask, he said quietly: "Because I love Chairman Mao."

He clearly did. This left a much more vivid impression with me than weeks of official propaganda.

ANTHONY GREY
Hostage in Peking, 1970

The xenophobic frenzy of the Cultural Revolution gradually gave way to a more pacific attitude toward the West, culminating in 1971 with "Ping-Pong diplomacy" — China's invitation to American table tennis players to compete in Peking. Then, in February 1972, President Richard M. Nixon made an unprecedented journey to China, ending twenty-two years of noncommunication between the two powers. For the eighty-seven-member U.S. press corps that accompanied the President, however, the twelve-day trip was a frustrating experience — an almost total black-out on substantive information left the newsmen scant news to report. The most interesting accounts of the journey turned up in journalists' personal impressions, such as the diary kept by Newsweek's *Washington bureau chief Mel Elfin.*

Sunday, Feb. 20

At first glance, China seems to come in four colors — yellow for the dusty earth, blue for the baggy clothing, red for the omnipresent slogans and gray for just about everything else. Yet China also looks as I had expected it to. Seemingly half the population wears gauze face masks as protection against cold, germs, dust and heaven knows what else. . . .

Monday, Feb. 21

In the pre-dawn darkness, I timidly venture forth on my first walk through Peking. From out of the gray haze, platoons of bicyclists silently pedal by on the way to work. There are no cars, rare buses and almost complete silence on a street as broad as the Champs-Elysées. If Fellini were to do a

Chinese movie, this would be his opening scene. In the afternoon, New York Timesman Max Frankel and I go shopping. As we walk up one of the large commercial streets, we realize that we are as much an object of curiosity to the Chinese as they are to us. After buying a few things, Max and I sit down for a luncheon snack at a primitive neighborhood cafeteria and between us spend 7 cents. Now, what accountant in the U.S. is going to believe that expense-account item: "Lunch, 3.5 cents"?

Tuesday, Feb. 22

At the Hsing Hua Hsi Li Housing Project, we find ourselves in a 10- by 16-foot room that is the home of Mr. and Mrs. Huang Hsu-fong and their three children. Aside from the obligatory portrait of Chairman Mao, a few pieces of furniture and a sewing machine, the room is bare. Yet Mrs. Huang is cheerful and friendly and claims to have no worries. As things turn out, she does have one worry — her son is not doing so well in school as his two sisters. We ask about the political meetings the Huangs say they hold nightly in their home. "We study the thoughts of Chairman Mao," says Mrs. Huang. "And what did you study last night?" we asked. "We didn't have a meeting last night," she says, "because my husband had to work late." Before leaving, I feel a tug at my elbow. Our guide says that the family that lives in the other room of the apartment would also like to be interviewed by the American journalists. We sense that the mood of formal hospitality has changed to warm friendliness.

Wednesday, Feb. 23

Her name is Pei Hsiao-rei, she's 25, highly intelligent and looks totally unlike my image of a Red Guard leader. Instead of being a cross between Bella Abzug and Madame Nhu, she radiates the softness of a Chinese version of the girl next door. Yet when the cultural revolution was at its fiercest, Miss Pei led a Red Guard faction at Peking University that broke up classes, destroyed countless books and art works and eventually forced the university to shut down. "The oppressed proletarian class in America will someday overturn U.S. capitalism," she says. How am I to explain to her that the working class in America has become the staunchest defender of the status quo?

Thursday, Feb. 24

Trooping atop the Great Wall with the President, I feel like an unpaid extra in a TV spectacular. So I return to the correspondents' bus and my mind turns to other things. I recall how at the gymnastics exhibition we saw last night, the audience applauded whenever a losing competitor tied up his match. "We applaud to encourage the underdog," said my guide. Knute Rockne would never have made it in China!

Friday, Feb. 25

Snow is falling and Peking looks a little less dreary. From my hotel window, I peer into the courtyard where two dozen men are sweeping, scraping and shoveling. All over Peking, armies of citizens are engaged in voluntary snow removal. So the city has no need for a sanitation department or snow blowers. Maybe John Lindsay should start studying Mao. Looking back over my stay in Peking, I realize that I have walked the darkest streets by night unafraid and left my hotel room unlocked without fearing for my possessions. I have not tipped a hotel employee or seen a beggar, a drunkard or a litterbug in the streets. But neither have I seen an attractively dressed citizen, or a dog, or heard an animated conversation.

159

Tomorrow I leave for home. Sitting in my Shanghai hotel room, I try to sort out my last impressions. In Hangchou, I saw the essence of southern China: the paddies, the exquisitely ordered landscape and the splendor of Chairman Mao's villa. Playing back the images, I wonder, can Maoism survive Mao? I think not. A people as imaginative as the Chinese cannot live permanently in drab regimentation. This was brought home to me at the ballet in Peking when a Western woman journalist entered, dressed in a dazzling silk blouse of ancient Chinese design. I saw the eyes of the women in the Mao jackets focus upon her until the curtain went up. That told me more about modern China than almost anything else.

MEL ELFIN
Newsweek, 1972

REFERENCE

Chronology of Chinese History

Entries in boldface refer to the Forbidden City

c.1766–1122 B.C.	Shang dynasty
1122–256	Chou dynasty
723–221	Yen dynasty, a Chou tributary, builds city of Chi on site of modern Peking
551–479	Life of Confucius
403–221	Warring States period
221–207	China unified for the first time by Ch'in dynasty; Chi becomes a provincial city
214	Great Wall completed
206 B.C.–A.D. 220	Han dynasty
220–589	Competing dynasties vie for control of China
589–618	Sui dynasty reunites empire and rebuilds Great Wall
605	Grand Canal completed
618–906	During T'ang dynasty, Chi renamed Yuchow
713–56	Cultural flowering during reign of Hsuan Tsung
755	Rebellion led by General An Lu-shan
907–59	Dissolution of empire following fall of T'ang
907–1125	Khitan Mongols, known as Liao dynasty, rule Yuchow region; capital renamed Yenching (Nanking)
960–1279	Sung dynasty reunites China; large areas of north remain under alien control
1115–1234	Chin dynasty establishes suzerainty over Sung
1153	Nanking rebuilt by Chin dynasty and renamed Chung-tu, "Central Capital"
1179	**Imperial palaces constructed at Chung-tu on site of modern Forbidden City**
1206	Genghis Khan unifies Mongol tribes
1215	Genghis Khan captures Chung-tu; fall of Chin
1260	Kublai, grandson of Genghis, assumes title of Great Khan of the Mongols
1264	Kublai moves Mongol capital to former Chung-tu; construction begun on new city on site, Ta-tu
1267	City walls of Ta-tu completed
1271	Mongols adopt Sinicized reign name of Yüan
1273–74	**Main halls of imperial palace of Ta-tu built**
1275–92	Marco Polo sojourns in China
1279	All of China brought under Yüan rule
1368	Hung Wu destroys Ta-tu, establishes Ming dynasty, and moves capital to Nanking; fall of Yüan
1404–20	**Reconstruction of Ta-tu, renamed Peking; building of Forbidden City is supervised by Yung Lo**
1421	Ming capital moved to completed Peking
1516	**State halls of Forbidden City rebuilt after fire**

1550–65	Southern suburbs of Peking walled in
1584–1626	Reign of Nurhachi, unifier of Manchu tribes
1572–1620	**Wan Li refurbishes buildings in Forbidden City**
1620–27	**T'ien-ch'i rebuilds palaces in Forbidden City destroyed by three major fires**
1636	Manchus adopt reign title of Ch'ing
1644	**Rebel Li Tzu-ch'eng seizes Peking and burns parts of Forbidden City;** last Ming emperor hangs himself; Manchus conquer city with aid of General Wu San-kuei and establish Ch'ing dynasty; **ruined palaces of Forbidden City rebuilt**
1645	**Three main halls of state in Forbidden City are renamed**
1648	Manchus confine their Chinese subjects to the southern section of Peking
1661–1722	Reign of K'ang-hsi, greatest Manchu emperor
1680	**Craft workshops established in Forbidden City**
1683	Taiwan incorporated as a Ch'ing prefecture
1699	**Hall of Supreme Harmony rebuilt**
1731	**Major earthquake damages Forbidden City**
1736–95	**Reign of Ch'ien Lung marks apex of Ch'ing power; library and retirement palace added to Forbidden City and many palaces are renovated**
1751	Manchus invade Tibet
1757	Manchus conquer Turkestan; all foreign trade confined to city of Canton
1765	**All three major audience halls repaired**
1793	Lord Macartney leads first British embassy to China
1797–99	**Three private halls of inner court of Forbidden City burned down and entirely rebuilt**
1839–42	Britain defeats China in Opium War
1842	By terms of Treaty of Nanking, Canton and Shanghai opened to trade; Hong Kong ceded to British; extraterritorial rights granted to foreign citizens
1850	Beginning of Taiping Rebellion
1853	Taipings capture Nanking
1858	Treaties of Tientsin open eleven new ports to trade; legations and missionaries authorized
1860	British and French troops occupy Peking; Summer Palace burned; first permanent British embassy established
1862–73	Tz'u Hsi becomes co-regent during minority of her son, boy-emperor T'ung Chih

1864	Nanking retaken; Taiping Rebellion crushed
1875–89	Second regency of Tz'u Hsi during minority of her nephew, emperor Kuang Hsü
1878	First Chinese ambassadors sent abroad
1887–89	**Renovation of Hall of Supreme Harmony**
1889	Kuang Hsü ascends throne
1890	**Repairs made on Gate of Supreme Harmony**
1894–95	Sino-Japanese War; China cedes Taiwan and suzerainty over Korea to Japan
1898	Kuang Hsü deposed and imprisoned following short-lived "Hundred Days" of reform; Tz'u Hsi resumes regency
1900	Boxer Rebellion; siege of foreign legations in Peking; allied armies occupy city; court flees
1902	Chinese government returns to Peking
1908	Death of Kuang Hsü and Tz'u Hsi; two-year-old P'u-yi named emperor
1911	Outbreak of Chinese Revolution
1912	Sun Yat-sen inaugurated as provisional president of the Chinese republic; abdication of the emperor, who continues to reside in the Forbidden City; **parts of Forbidden City nationalized and opened as a museum;** Yüan Shih-k'ai elected president
1915–16	Yüan Shih-k'ai fails to revive monarchy
1916–26	Civil war during warlord era
1919	Versailles Peace Conference awards German concessions in China to Japan
1921	First congress of the Chinese Communist party
1922	**Marriage of the emperor in the Forbidden City**
1923	**Emperor expels eunuchs from Forbidden City**
1924	Sun Yat-sen accepts Russian advisers and admits Communists to Kuomintang party; General Fêng Yü-hsiang captures Peking; emperor flees city
1925	Death of Sun Yat-sen
1926–28	Chiang Kai-shek, Sun Yat-sen's successor, leads Northern Expedition, defeats warlords, and nominally unites China
1927	Chiang Kai-shek establishes republic with Nanking as capital; massacre of Shanghai Communists; split develops between Communists and Nationalists
1928	Nationalists expel last warlord from Peking
1929	Skeletal remains of Peking man discovered

1930–32	Nationalist army fails to defeat Communists
1931	Mao Tse-tung establishes Communist government in Kiangsi; Japan occupies Manchuria
1934–35	Long March of the Communist army
1934	Henry P'u-yi, last of the Manchus, becomes puppet emperor of Japanese-dominated Manchukuo
1937	Japanese invade North China and seize Peking, Shanghai, and Nanking
1937–39	Nationalist and Communist forces form united front against Japanese aggression
1938–45	Japan controls northeastern third of China
1941–45	Communist guerilla action wins back large areas of Japanese-occupied northern countryside
1945	Japanese withdraw from China following defeat in World War II
1946	Civil war between Communists and Nationalists resumes
1948	**Communists take North China and Manchuria**
1949	Nationalist-held Peking surrenders to Communists; Mao Tse-tung proclaims People's Republic of China with capital at Peking; Nationalists withdraw to Taiwan
1950	Chinese "volunteers" intervene in Korean War
1950–57	Heyday of Sino-Soviet cooperation
1957	Temporary liberalization during "Hundred Flowers" period
1958	Great Leap Forward initiates intensive industrialization
1960	Split with Soviet Union
1966–67	Cultural revolution launched to purge "revisionism"; wave of terror led by Red Guards
1966	Death of P'u-yi, last emperor of China
1969	Border clashes with Soviet Union
1971	People's Republic admitted to United Nations
1972	President Nixon visits China
1973	**Construction begins on 20-story tourist hotel adjacent to perimeter wall of Forbidden City**
1976	Death of Mao Tse-tung
1980	Teng Hsiao-ping consolidates power; Maoist ideology seems to give way to modernization

The Great Wall

Snaking across China's northern landscape, over miles of mountain peaks and intervening valleys, the Great Wall stands as an immense monument to man's industry — and to his fears. Built in the third century B.C. to protect China's fertile plains from the marauding nomads of the northern steppes, the Great Wall stretches westward some 1,500 miles from the sea to the deserts of Sinkiang. Along that course it twists and turns back on itself so often that its actual length is almost double 1,500 miles — or roughly the distance from New York to Los Angeles. The wall's average height is twenty feet, and the road that runs along the top of it is wide enough to accommodate five horsemen riding abreast.

The Great Wall was built by China's first emperor, the tyrant Shih Huang Ti, who ruled from 221 to 210 B.C. Hundreds of miles of fortifications had already been built by various feudal chieftains to guard the mountain passes, but the new emperor, anxious to defend the whole length of his northern frontier, ordered that these sundry walls and watchtowers be joined together into one long rampart. Hundreds of thousands of laborers, guarded by an army of soldiers, were put to work on the wall. Slaves and scholars were added to the work force, together with hordes of "criminals" — people condemned for the most trivial offenses.

The work went on at a frantic pace, and the toll in human life and suffering was terrible. Watchtowers, as many as 25,000 of them, each built to house a hundred soldiers, were constructed within signaling distance of one another. Between the towers, walls were built of parallel courses of granite and brick and then were filled in with tamped earth.

In the end, the cost of supplying the multitude of laborers and troops needed to build and defend the wall helped to undermine Shih's empire. Even when partially garrisoned, however, his wall provided the farms and pasturelands to the south with a measure of security against foraging bands of nomadic warriors. As a modern historian has observed: "It is not easy to get horses over a twenty-foot wall, and still harder to make a rapid retreat with large flocks and herds of captured animals when such an obstacle lies in one's path." Although later generations cursed the tyrant's wall as an appalling waste of life and resources, the protection it afforded was appreciated by subsequent emperors, who diligently maintained the ramparts. Most of what remains of the wall today is the result of a rebuilding program undertaken during the Ming dynasty.

Valuable as the wall was in deterring isolated bands of horsemen, it had little effect once the nomads united under a strong leader. Time and again the stout garrison posts that guarded the mountain passes were overwhelmed, the Great Wall was breached, and the barbarian hordes, hungry for plunder, flooded into the fertile Chinese valleys. In the thirteenth century and again in the seventeenth they even established their own dynasties. Ironically, it was a barbarian dynasty, the Ch'ing (1644–1912), that finally made the borders of China secure. The Great Wall was gradually allowed to fall into disrepair, and today some sections in the far west are little more than piles of earth a few feet high. But hundreds of miles of wall remain — an awesome reminder of a turbulent history.

Guide to Other Monuments of China

Of all the monuments built in China for the glorification of the gods, the Temple of Heaven is probably the most beautiful and most perfectly formed. Indeed, it has been called "a masterpiece of human inspiration" and "the noblest example of religious architecture in the whole of China." Situated just inside the southern gate of Peking's outermost wall, directly across the Axial Way from the Temple of Agriculture, the Temple of Heaven balances the city astrologically as well as geographically. It provides the southern counterpart to the Altar of Earth on the north, the Altar of the Sun on the east, and the Terrace of the Moon on the west.

Begun by Emperor Yung Lo (1403–24)

and extensively restored in the eighteenth century, the Temple of Heaven lies within a 700-acre walled enclosure on grounds that were carefully laid out in accordance with ancient Chinese symbol and ritual. Standing at the southern end of the complex are the first of the temple's principal structures: a small round tower called the Temple of the God of the Universe; and the Altar of Heaven, a pyramid of three circular terraces ringed by marble balustrades and encompassed by a square courtyard. (In Chinese iconography the circular motif is symbolic of heaven, while the square symbolizes earth. Hence, as one approaches the altar one passes figuratively from earth to heaven.)

At the time of the winter solstice the emperor came to the Altar of Heaven, where he worshiped as high priest and intercessor for his people. He alone was privileged to ascend to the topmost terrace to offer sacrifice. Author Lin Yutang has written that "Heaven is the only God before whom the emperor bends his knee . . . and . . . this is the only time when he faces north to worship instead of facing south to receive worship."

In the early spring the prescribed rituals were performed at the opposite end of the complex, at the Hall of Prayer for Good Harvests. Here, on a date set by the court astronomers, the emperor prayed for a bountiful harvest. The structure itself is a magnificent round hall raised on three sacred terraces similar to those of the Altar of Heaven to the south. The temple's triple-tiered roof, covered with blue-glazed tiles, was formerly crowned with a gilded ball that glittered softly against the sky. Inside, the walls, beams, and pillars are richly painted in intricate patterns of red, blue, green, and gold. Visually, the temple dominates the complex, although the most important rites were actually performed at the Altar of Heaven.

With its geometric formality and majestic proportions, the landscape of the

Temple of Heaven is almost ethereal; it evokes a sense of transcendent grandeur that sets the spirit soaring. By contrast, the landscape of the Summer Palace is earthbound, sensuous, corporeal.

Located seven miles northwest of the Forbidden City, at the foot of the Western Hills, the Summer Palace and its grounds have been said to represent "the Chinese dream of an earthly paradise." High hills, meandering paths, cool lakes and streams, sudden vistas, tranquil glades — visual pleasures that nature would have spread over vast distances — are recreated in miniature within the park's 659 acres. In keeping with the Chinese ideal of an urban garden, the effect is one of calculated informality designed to soothe the troubled mind of the city dweller, to bring him face-to-face with nature while sparing him the difficulties of a long trip to the country.

Garden palaces have been built on this site ever since the twelfth century, but most of the present buildings and gardens were created in the 1880's and 1890's. At that time the empress dowager Tz'u Hsi decided to build a pleasure palace to replace the one that had been sacked and burned by European troops in 1860. Using funds earmarked for improving the antiquated Chinese navy — roughly fifty million dollars — she built a garden of unrivaled beauty and gave it its present name: the Garden Where Peace Is Cultivated.

The empress dowager's great palace, with its multitude of halls, chambers, and winding corridors, rises on successive levels from the southern slope of Longevity Hill, which overlooks a large lake that covers three-quarters of the palace grounds. Terraces and towers, carefully placed to capture the best views, dot the hillside. Along the shore, a beautifully painted, covered gallery winds among the trees for over half a mile, connecting the scattered palace buildings.

Nearby, on the northern shore of the lake, stands Tz'u Hsi's stone boat, an immobile two-story marble pavilion fitted with stone paddle wheels. The graceful Seventeen-arch Bridge, built in 1755, connects the mainland with the Island of the Dragon King. In still another corner of the lake rises the Jade Belt Bridge (also called the Camelback

Bridge), with its white marble balustrades. The waters of the Jade Fountain Spring — pure, cold, and emerald green — once flowed beneath it, but the spring has subsequently dried up.

On these bridges and along these garden paths the empress dowager spent her final days. Today the Summer Palace is a favorite playground of the people of Peking, who come for ice-skating in the winter and for swimming and boating in the summer.

Grandeur surrounded the Chinese emperors in death as well as in life, and the tombs of thirteen Ming emperors, lying in a beautiful valley twenty miles north of Peking, were designed to impress that fact upon all who came near. The valley, sheltered on three sides by mountains, is approached from the south along the Sacred Way, a long processional route lined with massive statues of horses, elephants, lions, camels, mythical beasts, and human figures. (The meaning of the statues is still a matter of conjecture; perhaps they were intended to serve the dead in the next world.) The Sacred Way leads to the

tomb of Emperor Yung Lo, builder of the Forbidden City and the Temple of Heaven, who chose this site in the early fifteenth century. All succeeding Ming emperors, with the exception of one, built their tombs nearby.

Yung Lo's tomb is by far the most impressive, the approach being marked by

a massive three-arched gate and by a succession of towers, halls, and beautifully landscaped courtyards. The great Hall of Eminent Favors, which stands in the midst of an enormous courtyard atop a triple terrace of white marble, is larger even than the palace halls in Peking. Beyond another courtyard is the entrance to the tomb itself, an artificial hill beneath which lie the remains of the Son of Heaven, his empress, and his second wife. The grave has not been opened, but in a nearby tomb archaeologists have found a veritable underground palace, its rooms furnished with funerary objects, gold ingots, porcelain vases, gold ornaments and headdresses, articles of clothing, and — beside an imperial coffin — twenty-six chests of treasure. Almost certainly the tomb of Yung Lo will one day yield even greater riches.

Selected Bibliography

Brake, Brian and Cameron, Nigel. *Peking: A Tale of Three Cities*. New York: Harper & Row, 1965.

Bretschneider, E. *Archeological and Historical Research on Peking and Its Environs*. Shanghai: American Presbyterian Mission Press, 1876.

Feng Yu-lan. *A History of Chinese Philosophy*, 2 vols. Translated by Derk Bodde. Princeton: Princeton University Press, 1952–53.

Giles, H. A. *A History of Chinese Literature*. New York: Grove Press, 1958.

Goodrich, L. Carrington. *A Short History of the Chinese People*. New York: Harper and Brothers, 1959.

Grousset, Rene. *The Rise and Splendor of the Chinese Empire*. Berkeley: University of California Press, 1953.

Latourette, Kenneth S. *The Chinese: Their History and Culture*. New York: Macmillan, 1946.

Li, Dun J. *The Ageless Chinese*. New York: Charles Scribner's Sons, 1965.

Needham, Joseph. *Science and Civilization in China*, 3 vols. Cambridge, England: Cambridge University Press, 1954–58.

Payne, Robert. *Portrait of a Revolutionary: Mao Tse-tung*. New York: Abelard-Schuman, 1961.

Reischauer, Edwin O. and Fairbank, John K. *East Asia: The Great Tradition*. Boston: Houghton Mifflin Company, 1960.

Snow, Edgar. *The Other Side of the River: Red China Today*. New York: Random House, 1962.

Terrill, Ross. *China: The 800 Million*. Boston: Atlantic-Little, Brown, 1971.

Willets, William. *Chinese Art*, 2 vols. London: Penguin Books Ltd., 1955.

(A complete, chapter-by-chapter bibliography is available upon request from the Newsweek Book Division, 444 Madison Avenue, New York, N.Y. 10022.)

Acknowledgments and Picture Credits

The Editors make grateful acknowledgment for the use of excerpted material from the following works:

An Embassy to China: Lord Macartney's Journal, 1793–1794. Edited by J. L. Cranmer-Byng. Copyright 1962 by J. L. Cranmer-Byng. The excerpt appearing on pages 95–98 is reproduced by permission of Longman Group Ltd.

China in the Sixteenth Century: The Journals of Matthew Ricci, 1583–1610. Translated by Louis J. Gallagher, S.J. Copyright 1953 by Louis J. Gallagher, S.J. The excerpt appearing on pages 139–40 is reproduced by permission of Random House, Inc.

The Confucian Persuasion edited by Arthur F. Wright. Copyright 1960 by the Board of Trustees of the Leland Stanford Junior University. The excerpt from the poem "Thinking About the Men of the Past Generation" by Cheng Ssu-hsiao appearing on page 64 is reproduced by permission of Stanford University Press.

Transactions of the American Philosophical Society, Volume 36 (1946). "History of Chinese Society" by K. A. Wittfogel and Feng Chia-sheng. The excerpt appearing on page 37 is reproduced by permission of the American Philosophical Society.

Hostage in Peking by Anthony Grey. Copyright 1970 by Anthony Grey. The excerpt appearing on pages 156–58 is reproduced by permission of Doubleday & Company, Inc.

Imperial Peking: Seven Centuries of China by Lin Yutang. Copyright 1961 by Lin Yutang. The excerpts appearing on pages 47 and 55 are reproduced by permission of Paul Elek Ltd.

Japan-China by Nikos Kazantzakis. Copyright 1963 by Simon and Schuster, Inc. The excerpt appearing on pages 155–56 is reproduced by permission of Simon and Schuster, Inc.

The Long March by Simone de Beauvoir. Translated by Austryn Wainhouse. Copyright 1958 by Simone de Beauvoir. The excerpt appearing on pages 153–54 is reproduced by permission of Ellen Wright.

Red Star Over China by Edgar Snow. Copyright 1938, 1944 by Random House, Inc. Copyright 1968 by Edgar Snow. The excerpt appearing on page 119 is reproduced by permission of Grove Press, Inc.

Sources of Chinese Tradition edited by William T. de Bary. Copyright 1960 by Columbia University Press. The excerpt appearing on page 92 is reproduced by permission of Columbia University Press.

The Travels by Marco Polo. Translated by Ronald E. Latham. Copyright 1967 by Ronald E. Latham. The excerpts appearing on pages 56 and 62 are reproduced by permission of Penguin Books Ltd.

Two Years in the Forbidden City by the Princess Der Ling. Copyright 1911 by Dodd, Mead & Company, Inc., renewed 1938 by the Princess Der Ling. The excerpt appearing on pages 147–48 is reproduced by permission of Dodd, Mead & Co.

Yuan Shih-k'ai by Jerome Ch'en. Second edition. Copyright 1961, 1972 by Jerome Ch'en. The excerpts on pages 115 and 118 are reproduced by permission of Stanford University Press.

The Editors would like to express their appreciation to Barbara Nagelsmith in Paris for her assistance. In addition, the Editors would like to thank the following organizations and individuals:

China Institute in America, New York
  Betty L. Schenck
Freer Gallery, Smithsonian Institution
  Thomas Lawton, Mary H. Quail
Mr. and Mrs. Rafi Y. Mottahedeh, New York
Museum of Fine Arts, Boston
  Lorraine Turner
National Palace Museum, Taipei, Taiwan
  Wang Chi-wu

Otto G. Nelson, New York
Princeton University
  Lucy L. Lo
Royal Ontario Museum
  Harold B. Burnham, Ursula Young
Thomas Froncek, New York
Lynn Seiffer, New York
Douglas Tunstell, New York
Wan-go H. C. Weng, New York

The title or description of each picture appears after the page number (boldface), followed by its location. Photographic credits appear in parentheses. The following abbreviations are used:

BN,P   Bibliothèque Nationale, Paris
BM   British Museum
FG   Freer Gallery, Smithsonian Institution
MMA   Metropolitan Museum of Art, New York
MFA,B Museum of Fine Arts, Boston

NPM   National Palace Museum, Taiwan,
         Republic of China
(PC)   (Private Collection)
(RTH) (Radio Times Hulton Picture Library)
ROM   Royal Ontario Museum

ENDPAPERS Painting of K'ang-hsi entering Peking, from *Panorama of Peking During the Celebration of the 60th Anniversary of the Chinese Emperor Ka-he's Birthday*, 1897. BN,P HALFTITLE Symbol designed by Jay J. Smith Studio FRONTISPIECE Carved lacquer box cover, Ming dynasty. ROM **9** Gold-and-turquoise *ju-i* from the desk of Ch'ien Lung, Ch'ing dynasty. FG **10–11** Palace of Supreme Harmony. (M. L. Maylin) **12–13** Ceiling in the Forbidden City. (PC)

CHAPTER I **15** Gilt statuette of a lion, T'ang dynasty. Victoria and Albert Museum **16** Detail from a handscroll of Yang Kuei-fei mounting a horse, by Ch'ien Hsuan, Yüan dynasty. FG **17** Detail from a handscroll depicting Hsuan Tsung, Ming dynasty copy. MMA, Kennedy Fund, 1913. **18** top, Pair of gold *apsarases*, T'ang dynasty. FG; bottom, Pottery tomb figure of a camel, T'ang dynasty. Collection of Mr. and Mrs. Rafi Y. Mottahedeh (Otto G. Nelson) **19** Hanging scroll depicting a palace, late Yüan dynasty. MMA, Rogers Fund, 1912 **20** Francis & Shaw, Inc. **21** Marble figure of a lion, T'ang dynasty. William Rockhill Nelson Gallery of Art **22–23** Detail from a handscroll of Liu Pang entering Ch'ang-an, by Chao Po-chu, Sung dynasty. MFA,B, William Gardner and Annie Hough Funds **24–25** left, Pottery tomb figure of a sheep pen, Han dynasty, c. 206 B.C. Victoria and Albert Museum; center, Pottery tomb figure of an oxcart, T'ang dynasty. MMA, Kennedy Fund, 1913; right, Pottery tomb figure of a watchtower, Han dynasty, 1–2nd centuries A.D.; bottom, Pottery tomb figure of a granary jar, late T'ang or Five Dynasties, 9–10th centuries. Everson Museum of Art, Cloud Wampler Collection. BM **26–27** left, Pottery figure of a warrior, T'ang dynasty. BM (Michael Holford); center, Bronze belt hook representing Han god of war, Later Han dynasty. FG; right, Painting of the Han palace, Sung dynasty, 12th century. NPM; bottom, Bronze tiger-shaped imperial message holder, Han dynasty. Collection of Mr. and Mrs. Rafi Y. Mattahedeh (Otto G. Nelson) **28** Francis & Shaw, Inc. **29** Stone relief of a warrior from the tomb of the T'ang emperor T'ai Tsung, 7th century. University Museum, Philadelphia **30** The Grand Canal. (PC) **31** Painting of the Grand Canal during the Sui dynasty, from *Traits . . . des Empereurs Chinois. . .*, 18th century. BN,P Oe 5 fol 11

CHAPTER II **33** Pottery tomb figure of a camel, Wei dynasty. MMA, Rogers Fund, 1928 **34–35** The Great Wall. (Henri Cartier-Bresson, Magnum) **36–37** Scroll of Tatars on horseback, by Li Tsanhua, Five Dynasties, 10th century. MFA,B, Keith McLeod Fund **38–39** top, Detail from a handscroll of a Mongol circus, by Chao Meng-fu, Yüan dynasty. 1254–1322. MMA, A. W. Bahr Gift, 1947; bottom, Detail from a scroll of the *Captivity of Wen Chi*, Sung-Ch'in dynasties, 12th century, MFA,B, Denman Waldo Ross Collection **40** Gold-and-jeweled burial crown, Sung dynasty. MMA, Fletcher Fund 1934 **40–41** top, Gold-and-jeweled hair ornament, Sung dynasty. ROM; bottom, Detail from scroll entitled *Life Along the River on the Eve of the Ch'ing Ming Festival* at Kaifeng, after Chang Tse-tuan, 12th century. BM **42–43** Details from the scroll *Life Along the River on the Eve of the Ch'ing Ming Festival* at Kaifeng, by Chang Tse-tuan. Peking Museum (Princeton University) **44–45** bottom, Painting of *Ladies Preparing Newly-woven Silk*, by Hui Tsung, Sung dynasty, 12th century; after Chang Hsuan, 8th century. MFA,B; top, Painting of *The Five-colored Parakeet*, by Hui Tsung, Sung dynasty, 12th century. MFA,B, Maria Antoinette Evans Fund **46** Francis & Shaw, Inc.

CHAPTER III **49** Pottery tomb figure of a horse's head, Han dynasty. MMA, Gift of Mrs. Samuel Peters, 1926 **50** Miniature of a Mongol battle, by Rashid al-Din, 1314. BN,P Supplement Persian, 1113, fol 155 **51** Miniature of the death procession of Genghis Khan, 16th century. BM, Ms. Or. 12998 fol 32 **52** Titlepage from edition of Marco Polo's memoirs, 1477. **54–55**

Three miniatures from *Le Livre des Merveilles*, by Marco Polo, 14th century. BN,P Ms. Fr. 2810, fol 5, 38 and 42 **57** The Bell Tower. (PC) **58–59** Detail from the Catalan Atlas, 1375. BN,P Espagnol 30 2v 3 **60** Francis & Shaw, Inc. **61** Album leaf of an imperial dragon boat, by Wang Chen-P'eng, 14th century. MFA,B **62** Portrait of Kublai Khan. NPM **63** Scroll of Kublai Khan hunting, by Liu Kuan-tao, Yüan dynasty. NPM **64–65** Handscroll entitled *Whiling Away the Summer*, by Liu Kuan-tao, Yüan dynasty. William Rockhill Nelson Gallery of Art **66–67** The Yangtze valley. (Marc Riboud, Magnum)

CHAPTER IV **69** Stone statue of a horse on the road leading to the Ming Tombs. (M. L. Maylin) **70** Painting of Emperor Shih Huang Ti burning books, from *Traits . . . des Empereurs Chinois . . .* , 18th century. BN,P Oe 5 fol 5 **71** Portrait of Hung Wu. NPM **72** Portrait of Yung Lo. NPM **73** Francis & Shaw, Inc. **74–75** left, Painting entitled *The Tejaprahba Buddha as Subduer of the Five Planets,* 897. BM, Stein Collection; bottom, Peking's axial way viewed from Coal Hill. (PC); right, Pottery tomb model of a residential compound, Ming dynasty ROM **76** South gate of the Forbidden City. (PC) **77** left, Dragon Pavement. (Norman Webb); right, Detail of the Dragon Pavement. (PC) **78** The Temple of Heaven. (PC) **80** Pottery tomb figure of a scholar-official, Ming dynasty. Everson Museum of Art, Cloud Wampler Collection **81** top, Carving of a philosopher in a landscape, Ming dynasty. Collection of H.M. the King of Sweden; bottom, Painting of candidates awaiting examination results, by Ch'iu Ying, Ming dynasty. NPM **82–83** left, Detail of two eunuchs from *Spring Morning in the Han Palace*, by Ch'iu Ying, Ming dynasty. NPM; right, Two vases showing ladies of the palace, Ming dynasty. Both: MMA, Gift of Edgar Worch, 1950 **84–85** left, Double-gourd enamel vase, Ming dynasty. Percival David Foundation; top and bottom, Two paintings entitled *Occupations of the Court Ladies*, after Ch'iu Ying, Ming dynasty, 16th century. Both: BM; right, Bamboo lacquered box with a scene of a palace audience, Ming dynasty, 17th century. M. H. De Young Memorial Museum, Avery Brundage Collection **86–87** Coal Hill. (PC) **88–89** The Meridian Gate and the River of Golden Water. (Marc Riboud, Magnum)

CHAPTER V **91** Wooden brushstand carved as a row of geese, Ch'ing dynasty. Everson Museum of Art, Cloud Wampler Collection **92** Roof detail from the Pavilion of Imperial Peace. (PC) **93** Guardian lions in the Forbidden City. (PC) **94–95** Three etchings of the summer palace at Jehol, by Matteo Ripa, 1713. Astor, Lenox and Tilden Foundations, New York Public Library **96** left, Brushpot from Ch'ien Lung's palace, Ch'ing dynasty; right, Hanging scroll of the Emperor Ch'ien Lung receiving the Portuguese ambassadors, Ch'ing dynasty. **97** top, Two carved wood-and-ivory figures of Europeans holding Buddhist symbols, from the imperial collection of the Emperor Ch'ien Lung. Ch'ing dynasty; bottom, Fan showing the foreign factories in Canton, c. 1775. Pages 96–97: Collection of Mr. and Mrs. Rafi Y. Mottahedeh (Otto G. Nelson) **98** Engraving of the west gate of Chinkiang, from *China* by Thomas Allom, 1842. **99** Opium smokers, c. 1880. George Eastman House **100–01** Detail from an album of paintings entitled *Imperial Troops Attacking a T'ai-p'ing Fort at Tientsin*. Chao-ying Fang Collection (Wan-go H. C. Weng) **103** Tz'u Hsi in her dragon robe. FG **104** The marble boat at the Summer Palace. (PC) **105** Nephrite vase from the Imperial Summer Palace, Ch'ing dynasty. MMA, Gift of Heber R. Bishop, 1902 **106** Phoenix robe from the wardrobe of Tz'u Hsi. ROM, Robert Simson Company **107** Silk rug from Ch'ien Lung's palace, Ch'ing dynasty. ROM, Bequest of Mrs. Frederick W. Cowan. **108** Two scenes of Chinese punishment. **109** center, Japanese executioner in China; right, Chinese victims of the Boxer Rebellion. Pages 108–9: George Eastman House **110** A throne room, Forbidden City. (Marc Riboud, Magnum)

CHAPTER VI **113** Figure of a turtle in the Forbidden City. (PC) **114** The Summer Palace (M. L. Maylin) **115** Lacquered panel with the *yin* and *yang* symbols. Wellcome Museum (Michael Holford) **116–17** left, P'u-yi (RTH); center, Gutted interior of Chang H'sun's palace, 1917. FG; right, Yüan Shih-k'ai (RTH) **118** Sun Yat-sen visiting the Ming Tombs outside Nanking. (RTH) **119** Sun Yat-sen's mausoleum. (M. L. Maylin) **120** Sun Yat-sen and his wife. (RTH) **121** Chiang Kai-shek and his wife. (RTH) **123** Kuomintang recruits in the courtyard of the imperial palace, 1949. (Henri Cartier-Bresson, Magnum)

CHAPTER VII **125** Guardian lion in the Forbidden City. (M. L. Maylin) **126–27** Parade in Tien An Men Square, October 1, 1970. (PC) **128** Mao Tse-tung. **129** Monument to the People's Heroes. (PC) **131** Lin Piao and Mao Tse-tung. **132–33** Fireworks in front of the Ch'ien Men, October 1, 1970. (PC) **134** Richard Nixon and Chou En-lai at the Peking airport 1972. (Wally McNamee)

THE FORBIDDEN CITY IN LITERATURE **136** Painting of guests arriving at the imperial palace, by Feng-Chi, c. 1500. BM **138–50** Eleven details from a handscroll depicting episodes from the lives of past emperors, by Li Kung-lin, Ch'ing dynasty. 17th century. All: FG **160** Calligraphy from *Thirteen Emperors Scroll,* by Yen Li Pen, T'ang dynasty. MFA,B Ross Collection

REFERENCE **164–65** The Great Wall. (PC) **166** left, The Temple of Heaven. (PC); right, Entrance gate to the Summer Palace. (PC) **167** left, The Seventeen-arch Bridge. George Eastman House; right, Road to the Ming Tombs. (M. L. Maylin)

Index

172